CONCEPTS IN SKILL LEARNING

CONCEPTS IN SKILL LEARNING

by
H.T.A. WHITING
M.A., Ph.D., F.B.Ps.S.
(Dept. of Physical Education,
University of Leeds)

LEPUS BOOKS
London 1975

Standard Book Number 86019 012 9

Computer Typesetting by Print Origination,
Bootle, Merseyside, L20 6NS
Printed and bound by Unwin Bros.,
Woking.

CONTENTS

ACKNOWLEDGEMENTS

G. Bell & Sons for permission to use material from
Morris, P.R. & Whiting, H.T.A. (1971) Motor impairment and compensatory education. (Section 5)
Whiting, H.T.A. (1969) Acquiring ball skills—a psychological interpretation (Sections 1 & 7)

The editor (R.A. Schmidt) of the Journal of Motor Behaviour for permission to reproduce Figs. 15, 16, 17 & 18, from the Journal in articles by the present author and his co-workers.

The editor Journal of Experimental Psychology for permission to reproduce Fig. 7 from an article by: Fleishman, E.A. & Hempel, W.E. (1955)

The editor South African Journal of Science for permission to reproduce Fig. 8 from an article by: Biesheuvel, S. (1963)

The material in Section 1 was published in *Research Quarterly,* **43**, 266-294. and that in Section 2 in *Sportswissenschaft,* **3**, 277-290.

INTRODUCTION

The more familiar we are with a process, the more we tend to take it for granted! While there would appear to be little point in paying undue attention to processes which only minimally effect our livelihood and well-being, it is surprising that the analysis of skilled behaviour has received comparatively little attention from experimental laboratories throughout the world.

At the stage when we were still a nation of craftsmen, when apprenticeships in the skilled trades were the norm, when son followed father into particular crafts and time for training was not at premium, there seemed to be little urgency about trying to understand the complex processes taking place as individuals moved from the unskilled towards the skilled end of the continuum. 'Sitting next to Nellie' seemed to be an appropriate way of training the novice through the expertise of the master. As recently as 1926, Book made the comment:

> Few systematic attempts have been made to determine and describe completely the psycho-physical habits of every kind and order involved in the acquisition of any special skill. And, so far as the writer is aware, no attempt has been made to determine just how these habits are acquired in the learning act. We do not know how any special school subject is actually learned or how any specific skill is acquired because no complete psychological history of their learning has been recorded.

Rapidly developing technology and preparations for conflict which have been so apparent in more recent decades—and which are not unconnected—have altered the picture. New technology demands new skills and its fast changing nature, the ability to transfer across tasks, acquiring new skills quickly and competently.

Involvement in war utilising modern technology not only demands the acquisition of many fundamentally novel skills, but it demands that they be acquired both quickly and efficiently. Training in high level skills becomes a central consideration with speed and efficiency at a premium. There is no time for extended apprenticeships, for 'sitting next to Nellie' procedures or the casual development of craftsmanship over an extended period. The demand is for skilled operators of sophisticated equipment—pilots, radar operators, gunnery experts, communication engineers etc. This was particularly true of the period during and immediately following the second world war which precipitated the current interest and acceleration of empirical work in the field of skill acquisition. The climate at that time is reported by Sir Frederick Bartlett (1958) who influenced this line of development in no small way:

> . . . the second Great War came, and for sufficient reasons my interests, and those of most of my colleagues, were diverted to experiments and reflections about bodily skill, its basic characteristics and the conditions of its acquisition and practice.

From such limited beginnings has developed an expanding body of literature in the form of books and specialist journals concerned with theoretical systems and constructs together with empirical evidence of a diverse kind. Not unnaturally, the early information in this field of study was fragmented in nature giving rise to discrete and disjunctive concepts largely devoid of unifying themes reflected not only in the literature but in the limited academic courses being offered to interested students. In this respect, in 1972, Gentile was moved to comment:

> The area of motor skills seemed to have a supermarket quality: a little massed/distributed practice here, feedback there, stacks of reaction time, mental rehearsal, speed/accuracy, short-term memory and other distinct topics of interest piled about in disarray. For the novice in the skills area, especially for the teacher-in-training whose entire experience may officially terminate with one undergraduate or graduate course, there seemed to be no need to selectively integrate the material into a package which could be easily handled and serve as a basis for future study or as a guide for operations performed by the teacher of skills.

Gentile's remarks were both apt and timely The student of perceptual-motor skill acquisition is not concerned with knowledge about isolated concepts derived from narrow laboratory procedures, but with the study of the development of highly organised, complex human behaviour involving the whole organism working as a coordinated unit (Whiting, 1972). Therein lies the problem—coming to terms with the complexity of behaviour which the expert skilled performer takes for granted.

The position that Gentile was rightly criticising is changing and changing rapidly as the attention of experimental psychologists and students of human movement in particular is increasingly being focused on that area of psychology which has come to be known as Human Performance and defined by Fitts and Posner (1967) as:

> . . . a branch of experimental psychology, analyses the processes involved in skilled performance, studies the development of skills and attempts to identify factors which limit different aspects of perform-ance. It seeks to analyse complex tasks into their simpler components and to establish quantitative estimates of man's abilities in each of the basic functions. In this way, it makes possible predictions about man's capability in performing complex skills.

This is the context in which this book is conceived Its purpose is to identify key concepts in skill acquisition and performance within a structured framework.

As might be expected when the topic of skilled *behaviour* becomes a central consideration, the majority of the evidence comes from the psychological literature. Limitations in this respect are reflected in an over-emphasis or *input* to the system—on man as a limited channel information processing system. This bias is being redressed and will be more so as interest in the phenomenon of skilled behaviour becomes a more central concern of other disciplines.

It might be asked whether the interest of psychologists in skilled behaviour is recent or whether it is only the rapid increase of interest which is noteworthy? The latter position would appear to be the case as there were certainly key figures from the psychology world making their contributions as early as the turn of the century. In fact, it would be true to say that much of the present integrated knowledge is based on ideas implicit in the work of such pioneers as Woodworth (1899), Bryan and Harter (1897; 1899) and Book (1925). More recently, the names of Bartlett (1947), Hick and Bates (1948), Fitts (1964) and Welford (1968) figure prominently in this area.

The present text owes much to the ideas of the people mentioned. It is intended as a source book for students but is by no means exhaustive of all the concepts in this area.

The book contains a collection of papers by the same author—some previously published in journals and some unpublished which together introduce the reader to many of the important concepts in skill learning. The sections do not necessarily follow on logically from one another, but there is sufficient overlap between the material presented to make each one an extension of concepts already introduced. A coherence will therefore emerge which is not necessarily apparent from the titles of the various sections.

In presenting what is after all only a selection from the total field, it is not possible to treat all the concepts in the same way or to the same depth. The result therefore reflects the particular biases of the author in work carried out prior to going to press. It will be apparent to the reader that the 'output' side of the skill model presented receives only superficial treatment. This is not to deny its importance but indicates that the constraints of a small book do not allow its development in depth.

The ideas reported in this book owe much to discussion and elaboration with my doctoral students, John Alderson, Ian Cockerill, Lesley Cooke, Brian Hopkins, Mary Kenchington, Frank Sanderson, Bob Sharp, and Dave Tyldesley. I am pleased to be able to acknowledge my debt in this respect.

Leeds
January 1975   H.T.A. Whiting

References

BARTLETT, Sir F. (1958). *Thinking—an experimental and social study.* London: Unwin.

BOOK, W.F. (1926). *The psychology of skill with special reference to its acquisition in typewriting.* London: Gregg Publishing Co.

BRYAN, W.L. & HARTER, N. (1897). Studies in the physiology and psychology of the telegraphic language. *Psychol. Rev., IV,* 27.

BRYAN, W.L. & HARTER, N. (1899). Studies on the telegraphic language: the acquisition of a hierarchy of habits. *Psychol. Rev., VI,* 345-375.

FITTS, P.M. (1964). Perceptual-motor skill learning. In A.W. Melton (Ed.) *Categories of human learning.* New York: Academic Press.

FITTS, P.M. & POSNER, M.I. (1967). *Human Performance.* Belmont: Brooks/Cole.

GENTILE, A.M. (1972). A working model of skill acquisition with application to teaching. *Quest,* 17, 3-23.

HICK, W.E. & BATES, J.A.V. (1948). The human operator of control mechanisms. Ministry of Supply permanent records of Research and Development, No. 17.

WELFORD, A.T. (1968). *Fundamentals of skill.* London: Methuen.

WHITING, H.T.A. (1972). Theoretical frameworks for an understanding of the acquisition of perceptual-motor skill. *Quest,* 17, 24-34.

WOODWORTH, R.S. (1899). The accuracy of voluntary movement. *Psychol. Rev. Monog. Suppl.,* 3, No. 3.

1

AN OVERVIEW OF THE SKILL LEARNING PROCESS

1 AN OVERVIEW OF THE SKILL LEARNING PROCESS

In classifying some observed behaviour as 'skilled', it is being distinguished from other behaviour which is in some way 'unskilled'. At an everyday level, the terms skilled and unskilled *labour* are used to differentiate between those members of the community who have had successful specialised training in a particular industrial skill(s) and those who have not. Thus, a continuum 'skilled-unskilled' is a simple but useful way of classifying behaviour. The learning process on which this overview centres is concerned with progression along the continuum from being unskilled to becoming skilled.

It might be asked whether such a continuum could usefully be applied to *all* behaviour, or whether it is inappropriate (because for example of the simplicity of the stimulus response (S-R) sequence involved) to label certain behaviour as skilled or unskilled. Such a question is concerned with the criteria on which skilled behaviour is assessed.

Complexity of behavioural response

The continuum skilled-unskilled, would only appear to be used in relation to relatively *complex* behaviour, which is emitted in an attempt to bring about a successful outcome to some predetermined objective. To some extent, this still begs the question as there remains the difficulty of defining what is meant by *complex*. This cannot be done in a definitive way, the cut-off point between what is simple and what is complex being an arbitrary one.

Bartlett (1958) for example points out that the term 'skill' is not usually used in connection with acts of behaviour such as those involved in linking a simple stimulus to a simple response. He cites as examples *simple* reaction-time S-R sequences and laboratory investigations of threshold values in psychophysical experiments in which learning plays a very limited part. While such acts fulfil one of the criteria of skilled behaviour—*the successful*

3

achievement of a predetermined end result—they are better conceived as component parts of more complex behavioural responses. It is the sequential organisation of such simple components and their hierarchical structuring in bringing about a successful outcome which constitutes skilled behaviour.*

More recently, Renshaw (1974) points out that:

> . . . an important distinction has to be drawn between those mindless physical movements that just happen to us, such as nervous twitches and reflex movements, and those consciously conceived actions which presuppose the rational formulation of intentions within a particular frame of reference.

Intention

Whatever processes may be involved in *human* skill learning and performance, the concern is with *intentional* attempts to carry out motor acts which will bring about predetermined end results. The concept of *intention* as one of the criteria of skilled behaviour is an important one, because the instinctive behaviour—involving 'fixed action patterns' (Lorenz, 1937; Tinbergen, 1942)—of animals often involves behavioural repertoires which are apparently quite complex but they are not generally looked upon as examples of *skilled* behaviour. Such innately determined responses are *elicited* by appropriate environmental cues ('releasers'). As such they are to be differentiated from the intentional behaviour of man involved in the learning and performance of *a skill*. Such a distinction is also made in learning theory between the *elicited* responses of classical conditioning and responses which are *emitted* in instrumental conditioning (Skinner, 1961).

Learning

One of the criteria which differentiates the kind of complex behaviour which it is wished to designate as skilled from other complex forms of behaviour such as 'fixed action patterns' is the time-course of the learning process. Progress along the continuum from unskilled to skilled generally involves a *protracted* period of learning. Thorpe (1964) makes a useful differentiation in this respect:

---

*In Fitts and Posner's (1967) computer analogy terms, skilled behaviour would involve the effective ordering and hierarchical structuring of sub-routines. In a similar way, Miller, Galanter and Pribram (1960) discuss elemental TOTE units becoming organised through learning into complex behavioural repertoires.

The best method of approach is to consider the origin of behaviour complexity. Where does the complexity of the behaviour come from? If we can see the necessary complexity in the input from the environment which is being, or has previously been, experienced, then we are justified in assuming provisionally that it has been learned. If, however, there is complexity in the behaviour pattern which is not seen in the immediate, or indeed the whole, previous experience of the individual animal, then we have to assume that this complexity comes from somewhere else and that it can only have come from the inborn organisation of the animal.

Skilled behaviour which brings about a predetermined end result is therefore on the above criteria, *learned* behaviour; it is *complex* behaviour in terms of the sequential and hierarchical ordering of simple response units (sub-routines, TOTE units etc.) and it is *intentional.* Such complex behaviour relates to the performance of *a skill* which in this context can be looked upon as *a predetermined end result.* The difficulty in being precise about the latter is evidenced in the fact that the predetermined end result by which specific skills are defined may be:

(i) independent of the way in which they are achieved (in the sense of a definitive movement pattern).
(ii) solely in terms of prescribed movement patterns.
(iii) a combination of both criteria.

The difficulty in this respect is discussed in detail in Section 2.

Definitions of skill

To be *skilled* then, is to be proficient in the performance of *a skill.* The kind of criteria discussed above have led Knapp (1964) extrapolating from the work of Guthrie (1952) to propose the following definition of *skill:*

... the learned ability to bring about predetermined results with maximum certainty often with the minumum outlay of time or energy or both.

Argyle and Kendon (1967) focus attention on different criteria:

An organised co-ordinated activity in relation to an object or a situation which involves a whole chain of sensory, central and motor mechanisms ... the performance is continuously under the control of the sensory input . . . which controls the performance in the sense that outcomes of actions are continuously matched against some criterion of achievement or degree of approach to a goal according to which the performance is corrected.

Here, Argyle and Kendon are stressing *complexity* in terms of the many processes involved, together with the importance of *negative feedback* (the discrepancy between some internalised model or template of the skill to be carried out and the current attempt at such a skill) which is necessary for the refinement of the skilled behaviour.

Since either of these definitions alone fails to stress some of the above criteria, the following composite definition of *skilled behaviour* is proposed:

Complex, intentional actions involving a whole chain of sensory, central and motor mechanisms which through the process of learning have come to be organised and co ordinated in such a way as to achieve predetermined objectives with maximum certainty.

Classification of skills

Without at this stage becoming involved in the complexities of skill classification, several broadly defined categories can be distinguished. Thus, verbal, mental, perceptual, social and motor are common adjectives in relation to skills. It would however be wrong—as the above definition implies—to assume that the processes involved in the learning of any of these skill categories is essentially different from the learning of another. In many ways for example—and particularly from an explanatory point of view—the designation *motor* skills or *perceputal* skills are misnomers since it would be difficult to think of any related skilled behaviour in which only efferent or only afferent processes were involved. Fitts and Posner (1967) distinguish between:—

1 Perceptual-motor skills
2 Language skills

but at the same time recognise that both categories involve perceptual and motor abilities. Welford (1968) suggests that a distinction is commonly drawn between sensory-motor and mental skills but that such differentiation is difficult to maintain completely. The subject is further complicated by Elkind and Weiss' (1967) contention that patterns of visual exploration (which might normally be classified as perceptual learning) are in effect, motor skills. Gibson (1968) has also pointed out that man is not a static receiver of stimulation but an active, aggressive seeker of environmental information. In discussing the senses as perceptual-systems, he suggests that such systems are orientated in the appropriate way for the assimilation of environmental information and that such a procedure depends upon the orientation of the whole body. Such orienting responses can then be considered as examples of skilled behaviour and their acquisition interpreted in a similar way to that of any other skills. It might well be that an early stage in skill learning is the acquisition of sub-skills concerned with 'getting the idea of the orientation required in order to be capable of 'picking-up' the appropriate environmental information on which the control of the skill depends' (Whiting, 1972).

Models of Skilled Behaviour

One of the anomalies in the acquisition of skill, is that on the one hand, the *complexity* of the procedure is being stressed while on the other, the highly skilled person's behaviour is often described as effortless, polished, smooth, beautifully-timed etc. giving the impression of *simplicity*. It is only when an awareness of the difficulties involved in passing from the 'unskilled' to the 'skilled' category are appreciated that the immense complexity of the problem is realised. One of the reasons why many highly skilled people are poor teachers of such skills is a lack of such awareness.

The student of skill acquisition is concerned with the study of the development of highly organised, complex human behaviour involving the whole person functioning as a co-ordinated unit. Any framework which will aid in the understanding of such a complex procedure, which will prove of heuristic value and which in itself is not so over-simplified as to prove facile is to be welcomed. A number of different models of skilled behaviour have been proposed over the years and these have been categorised by Fitts (1964) as follows:

1 Communication models based on the coding, translation, transmission and storage of data.
2 Control system models—the regulation of behaviour through the interplay of input, output, feedback and 'noise' variables; cybernetic theory with particular emphasis on self-regulating closed-loop systems.
3 Adaptive system models based on the existence of hierarchical processes and analogous to computer operations with low and higher order programmes or routines.

Since all of these models have something to contribute to the understanding of the processes involved in skill acquisition, it would obviously be helpful to keep them all in mind. What does however seem clear, is that consideration of the human organism as an information-processing system with limited channel capacity (Welford, 1968) has proved to be the most fruitful line of enquiry. The fact that difficulties have been encountered in generalising from a theory (information theory—Cherry, 1957) developed in the context of more mechanistic communication systems is perhaps not surprising. Nevertheless, as Broadbent (1965) point out:

> In the general sense therefore the use of information theory has produced a revolution in psychological thought whose full consequences have not yet been digested; although experiment has disproved naive ideas of a simple representation of the nervous system as a single-channel needing no further analysis.

For these kinds of reason, it is proposed to present a basic model for an understanding of skilled behaviour which owes much to the work of Broadbent (1958), Crossman (1966), Fitts (1964) and Welford (1968) as a first stage and then to elaborate some of its weaknesses and considerations which have to be borne in mind in developing such a *systems* model. The static two-dimensional model presented would be classified under Fitts' category of communication system models. But, even at this stage such a limitation must be overcome by conceiving of the model as a dynamic three-dimensional one in which continual elaboration is taking place. Such a conception is that of an adaptive system.

Systems-analysis of perceptual-motor skill performance

A systems-analytic approach to model building attempts to establish sub-systems on the basis of structural or functional similarities and to relate these to the functioning of the system as a whole. In terms of the physical components of human perceptual-motor skill performance, three major sub-systems are apparent (Fig. 1):

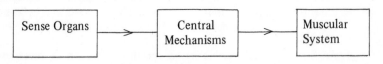

Fig. 1. Physical Components.

which at a functional level are responsible for input to the system decision-making and output (Fig. 2):

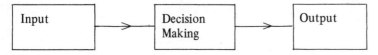

Fig. 2. Functional Components.

At a more complex level of analysis, the central mechanisms may be considered to carry out three major functions—perception, translation and effector control (Fig. 3):

Fig. 3. Central Mechanisms.

These three sub-analyses can be incorporated into a composite model (Fig. 4):

Such a model may be found useful in understanding the processes which take place during skill acquisition and performance.

At a simple level, information from the display (immediate external environment in which the skill is to be carried out) is necessary for the control of the developing skilled behaviour although the importance of such information will depend upon the task in hand and the stage of learning reached. For some skills, such information will be of primary importance while for others, its purpose may be simply that of indicating to the person performing the skill, where or when it is to be carried out (e.g. (1) In a shot put circle, (2) At 6.30 a.m. sound the bugle call), its use in the actual control of the movement being minimal. In this respect, Knapp (1964) extrapolating from the work of Poulton (1957) has proposed a skill classification on a continuum ranging from *open* to *closed* depending upon the extent to which control of the skilled behaviour is determined by external rather than proprioceptive information.*

Selection of Input

In any skill learning/performance situation, the display ('input space' in Moray's (1969) terms) resonates with *potential* information. Because of the

---

*The limitations of such a continuum are discussed in Section 2.

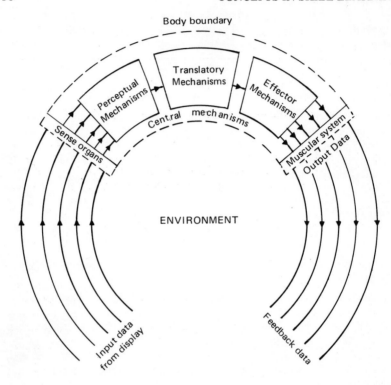

Fig. 4. Systems analysis of perceptual-motor skill performance. (Whiting, 1969)

limited capacity of the nervous system (Broadbent, 1965) it is not possible to utilise *all* the potential information in the display and in any case, much of this information will be of little value in controlling the skilled behaviour. Experience within the skill-learning/performance environment leads to an appreciation of the *constancies* in the situation. That is to say, those aspects of the environment which convey little information which is going to be useful in controlling the skilled behaviour. Such information is redundant. It tells the performer something which he already knows and hence at the most is confirmatory. More concern is with the unpredictable events because in the first place it is more difficult to allow for such exigencies (in view of the amount of information (in an information theory sense*) they contain) or in

---

*In such a context, information is defined as that which removes uncertainty. Thus, the greater the 'surprise' value of an event, the *more* information it contains because when it has happened it removes more uncertainty.

allowing for them, a certain amount of the individual's channel capacity must be held available for dealing with such information. Learning what information in the display is worth having or not worth having and what part of the display to orientate towards, involves the processes of selective attention/ orientation/perception.

Selective attention/orientation/perception

The need to take in information from the environment, inevitably raises the question of the focusing of *attention*. Although such a problem must be a relatively old one, it would appear to have received more explicit formulation and experimentation at the turning point of modern psychology. Titchener (1901) in making this proposal, defined attention—in short—as a 'state of consciousness'. This emphasis was reflected in the introspective experimental approach which was applied to the phenomenon at the time. He elaborated further the difficulties involved when he discussed the ways in which attention has been regarded at various times:

> . . . as a peculiar power of capacity, the 'faculty of concentration', the ability to restrict at will the field of consciousness, as a peculiar form of mental activity, an effort which one puts forth or an initiative which one takes, so contradistinguished from the passivity with which perceptions and ideas are received; as a state of the whole consciousness, a state of clear apprehension and of effective thought; as a feeling or emotion and finally as a sensation complex running its course alongside of the other mental processes, perceptions, feelings etc. of the attentive consciousness.

It is interesting to note in the light of these statements the more recent suggestions by Posner and Klein (1974) that consciousness is related intimately to the operations of the limited capacity mechanism discussed below.

One of the difficulties implicit in developing the concept of attention is the subjective element involved As Stout (1899) pointed out many years ago, attention is always in a way expectant or prospective:

> To attend is always to watch to wait, to be on the alert and preadjusted for what is coming.

Individual differences in this respect are to be expected.

In current terms Stout's concept would probably be classified as 'general attention' which is related to the concept of *activation and arousal* (discussed below). Adams (1966) elaborates this point in suggesting that the layman's criterion of attention is reflected in the physiologist's contention that when the reticular formation of a quiescent or sleeping animal is stimulated, he assumes postural alertness—pricks up his ears and looks around in a manner that has come to be recognised as being attentive. This again is reminiscent of Woodworth and Schlosberg's (1963) differentiation of *free* attention from that of *controlled* attention. In the former, there is no assigned task and the question is simply which of the stimuli will 'catch the attention' and elicit the selective response.

Currently, much experimental work is being focussed on the physiological correlates of attention and particularly on variations in E.E.G. recordings from the scalp. Such recordings are used to detect signs of evoked responses to sensory stimuli. In this respect, Wilkinson (1967) refers to non-specific and specific characteristics of the evoked response. The former—which can be recorded from many parts of the scalp—responds to changes in the general attentional state of the person (already discussed) and the latter—found over the primary projection areas of the sensory modes concerned—reflects response to specific stimuli. Van Olst et al (1967) distinguish between 'tonic' and 'phasic' arousal. Tonic arousal being an organismic state of vigilance of relatively permanent character (general attention?) and phasic arousal a respondent state of vigilance increment of short endurance and dependent upon the stimulus conditions. In practice of course there is a functional interaction between the two.

Such comments on general or free attention are useful to describe phenomena which are known to exist, but it is the phasic or specific part of the evoked response which is of major importance in the present context. Horn (1965) clarifies the above difficult concepts in a more specific way when he suggests that:

> ... an organism is said to attend to a stimulus when it makes some behavioural or perceptual response to that stimulus

and,

> ... when the stimulus is chosen for response out of a constellation of stimuli falling on the sense receptors, the organism is said to show evidence of selective perception.

Similar difficulties to those already encountered with respect to attention arise with respect to the concept of orientation. Gibson (1968)—in discussing the senses as perceptual systems—suggests at one stage that such systems are orientated in the appropriate way for the pickup of environmental information and such a procedure depends upon the general orientation of the whole body. The *general* nature of such a process is further reflected in his statement that perceptual systems:

> ... serve to explore the information available in sound, mechanical contact, chemical contact, and light.

However, in a more specific way he contends that:

> ... the animal adopts temporary orientations to events and objects whenever he attends to them.

Now, if—as has been contended above—attention is always *to* something it would seem logical to accept that orientation is always *to* something. Obviously one cannot pick up visual information unless the eyes are orientated towards the appropriate part of the display.

The skill performer cannot utilise *all* the potential information available in a display and as previously suggested, much of this information will be of little value in controlling the skill. For these reasons, and because in many skills there is only a limited time available in which to take in information, he needs to be selective. That is to say, the performer needs to know to what part of the display his perceptual systems—in Gibson's terms—must be orientated (an efferent process) and what information to abstract from that part of the display on which attention is focused (an afferent process). Gibson (1968) has clarified this further in distinguishing between overt or *external* attention in the manner described above as an *efferent* process and *covert* attention (internal) which Broadbent (1958) has conceived of as a filtering of the input information at various centres of the nervous system. It is to this form of attention that major experimental work in recent years has been directed. This work will be discussed later in this section.

The difficulties inherent in this procedure of selective attention would be determined in a skill situation by such factors as:

1 The *ability* of the performer to selectively attend to the most useful source of information or in some instances to *vary* his attention in a systematic way i.e. scanning the display in the most efficient manner.

2 The total amount of information in the display. Some displays for example may be so structured that it is virtually impossible to take out the wrong information. Deliberate structuring of such a situation may in fact be an important *ergonomic* consideration. Although one of the objectives of the ergonomist may be that of preventing the display from being confusing, it is worth noting that in competitive games (for example) players may do their utmost to confuse the

display for the opposition thus making the abstraction of the relevant information more difficult.

Focusing attention on a small part of the display with the objective of perceptual clarity may not always be desirable. Sometimes, it is useful for attention to be diffused over a wide area such that while no one part of the display will be clearly perceived, the performer may have a general awareness of the whereabouts of particular sources of information (Vernon, 1962). On occasions, a person may—after a diffuse appraisal—be aware that something is different in a situation but will not be sure what until a more detailed examination of the display has been made. The latter may not always be necessary since the former may be sufficient information on which to make a decision.

3 The time available. In some skills (e.g. fast ball games) there is comparatively little time in which to take in the information required so that there is little margin for error, while in others, sampling the input can be spread over a considerable amount of time. It is obvious that in situations where time is limited it will be necessary to concentrate attention accurately on the critical area of the display and to be 'set' (Stout's 'expectancy') to perceive a particular kind of information as quickly and accurately as possible. One of the problems in becoming a skilled performer is concerned with learning to do just that! In fact, one of the criteria on which a teacher, trainer or coach might be judged successful, is his ability to make his trainee's attention selective by pointing out that part of the display towards which his perceptual systems need to be orientated and the information he is to try to abstract. Unsophisticated teachers may fail to appreciate that the beginner in a skill may not be utilising the same information as the expert and in consequence may try to extrapolate from what the expert is known to do, to what the beginner ought to do. Breakdown in training procedures under such conditions are likely (Whiting, 1969).

Filtering

The idea of a *covert* form of selective attention implies that once one or more of the perceptual systems have been orientated towards a particular part of the display with the object of picking up information further selection from amongst such information takes place resulting in a limited amount of information being available to the person for the purpose of making a response. Such a selection or filtering procedure serves to limit the possibility of overloading the limited channel capacity of the human organism and at a more extreme level ensures that the brain itself is not continuously bombarded by diffuse sensory input much of which will carry redundant information and may lead to excessive arousal. In addition, the processing of unnecessary (to the task in hand) information may lead to delays in decision-making necessary for adaptive behaviour.

Thus, there would appear to be two main reasons why filtering should take place:

1 so that the information processed should be only that which makes subsequent behaviour adaptive
2 the prevention of overactivation of the sensory cortex in the form of excessive bombardment of the brain by afferent impulses.

The question now is how specific information is selected from the sensory input and how such selection is influenced by prior experience (memory stores)?

Selective orientation in itself is not sufficient, as the amount of information falling on the sensory receptors will still be very large. In addition, orientation does not necessarily imply perception. Adams (1966) has made this point clearly:

Because of these various differences between looking and seeing—between being merely orientated to a stimulus and discriminating it—I think that we must throw our weight in the direction of seeing or, more generally, the observing response, which not only implies receptor orientation but also stimulus reception and discrimination for the criterion response that follows. . .

Difficulties of this nature have been apparent in work carried out on eye-movement recording. Although the sophisticated techniques adopted enable a fairly accurate measure of where the eye is looking, there is no guarantee that information from the display (particularly that in which the experimenter may be interested) is being taken in.

From the developing work in this area, it would appear likely that the processes of the central nervous system which are influenced by memories, emotional states etc. can facilitate or inhibit sensory input patterns by means of systems of fibres that run from the brain to synaptic regions in the afferent pathways (Livingston, 1959; Melzack, 1968). These may not be the only filter mechanisms. Marler (1961) for example has proposed three types of filtering system:

1 that imposed primarily by the receptors (on the basis of their physical structure or biases which have been imposed by facilitatory

or inhibitory feedback mechanisms from the C N S). In addition, there are indirect effects like changes in the size of the pupil of the eye or tensions in the muscles which adjust the eardrum (Broadbent, 1965).

2 by the receptor afferent pathways and the C N S as they function together in normal perception.

3 by a *central* filtering mechanism

Welford (1968) has however argued that experimental findings may be capable of interpretation in terms of one filter system in the perceptual mechanisms themselves.

The concept of sensory filtering is not new. Major developments in this area would appear to have been brought about by the work of Broadbent (1958) and Cherry (1957).

Broadbent's (1958) earlier work led him to postulate a filter mechanism existing between the sense organs and the central mechanisms which would allow only signals with particular physical characteristics or from particular sense organs to be relayed further. Developing work in this area led to the suggestion that an interpretation of this nature was too narrow and that there must have been some prior analysis of the data before selection was made (Broadbent, 1966).

That the amount of information available to the person is greater than normally anticipated has been demonstrated in an ingenious series of experiments by Averbach and Sperling (1960). They showed a major limiting factor in the use of such information to be short-term memory decay. Instead of presenting subjects with a series of letters or figures for recall some short-time afterwards (as is often the case in measuring the memory span) these workers presented their subjects with for example three rows of letters and immediately afterwards indicated which of the three rows was to be recalled. The experiment indicated that subjects had a larger span of attention than had previously been realised and also that such information if not rehearsed, decays rapidly with time. Thus, the limitation did not lie in the perceptual systems themselves, but in the central mechanisms concerned with identifying and reporting the stimuli.

Habituation

Another kind of selectivity is operating in cases of habituation—the decrease or disappearance of a response to a stimulus which is presented repeatedly (Treisman, 1966). As might be expected in many skill learning/ performance situations (particularly 'open' skills in Knapp's terminology) the stimulus subsets carrying the information which is important or essential to carrying out the task must be discriminated from all the other stimulus subsets whose potential information is not necessary to the task in hand. That is to say, that the skill performer must learn to habituate to such unnecessary stimulation so that 'he no longer notices the events *constant* to this particular task in the environment' (Pribram, 1966). In skills which take place in a relatively constant environment such a procedure will presumably be much easier than those which take place in a relatively changing environment. In the latter case, the performer has to learn to habituate to many more different stimulus subsets in the varying display. Pribram further suggests that in habituating to a stimulus subset the subject no longer produces an orienting reaction in as far as he will fail to move his head and eyes in the direction of the stimulus, will show characteristic electrophysiological measures implying absence of phasic arousal and if called upon to report verbally on the situation will indicate that he is not attending.

Limits of Attention

Earlier in this section, it was suggested that the sheer quantity of information available in a display generally made selectivity an essential procedure. It might now be asked what limits are imposed upon attention? At a subjective level it will be appreciated that as a person becomes more skilled at a particular skill he needs to give less attention both to the display and the actual initiation of the response. He is said to perform autonomously (Fitts and Posner, 1967). The difference is well illustrated in comparing the ability of a learner driver to perform effectively while listening to the radio as compared with an experienced driver. More interference is likely to occur in the former instance but the experienced driver is also likely to suffer some deficit. This might be explained in terms of information processing. It would be assumed that the learner driver needs to process more information—since he will be unsure of what information is worth having—and therefore has less channel capacity available to deal with extraneous sources of information. The amount of interference in the example quoted will depend upon what information is coming over the radio and what response the driver is required to make to such information. Thus, the limits imposed upon attention would appear to be in terms of the information content of the display and the limited channel capacity of the performer (Treisman, 1966).

In these terms, if a subject is required to pay attention to one or more input channels and the information content of the 'attended' channel is sufficient to occupy all or most of his attention, little can be recalled of information coming in on the other channels.

Two main groups of theories have been put forward to account for the nature of the selectivity process (Norman, 1969):

1 Early selection theories (Broadbent, 1958; Treisman, 1960; Treisman and Geffen, 1967) in which it is proposed that initial selection is based on the physical properties of the impinging stimulus energy and only those signals so selected are perceived (in terms of a meaning being extracted).

2 Late selection theories (Deutsch and Deutsch, 1963; Norman, 1969) implying that all incoming stimulus energy undergoes a preliminary analysis and that selection then takes place in terms of both the physical properties of the stimulus and its meaning.

The latter theory implies that every stimulus presented must be analysed through permanent memory and must also be briefly available in short term memory. This would mean that something could be remembered of all events—even those not attended to. While much of the current literature argues against such an interpretation, Norman (1969) has recently demonstrated that some of the difficulty in interpretation can be accounted for in terms of the methodology employed. Thus, he was able to show that if subjects were tested for retention on non-attended channels *immediately* after the presentation of a stimulus set (instead of after an appreciable delay as occurs in most of the experimental literature) they did in fact recall an appreciable amount of the content. He interprets these results as showing that verbal material presented on non-attended channels gets into short-term memory but is not transferred into long-term memory. These findings open up new considerations in the area of selective perception.

'Activation' and 'Arousal'

The need to consider the model proposed for perceptual-motor skill performance as a *dynamic* model has already been stressed. In addition to the context in which this idea was discussed, it will be appreciated that incoming sensory information (in the form of neural coding) is not projected onto an inert and inactive cortex. The cortical system is always to some degree 'activated' or 'aroused'. Although these two terms are generally used synonymously, Eysenck (1968) prefers to differentiate between *autonomic* 'activation' and *cortical* 'arousal'. Initially a distinction will not be maintained but Eysenck's dichotomy will be developed later in the section.

The concept of 'activation' is not in itself a new one. It is related in many ways to earlier concepts of motivation, energisation, and generalised 'drives'. The latter term implies a behaviour 'energiser' but is not concerned with the directional guidance of behaviour so energised. In a similar way, arousal apparently has no steering function in behavioural control. An activated or aroused organism is said to be *attentive* in terms of a general postural alertness. While a useful description of manifested reaction the possible confusion in such terminology was discussed in the section on selective attention.

Duffy (1932) was one of the early workers in this field, before the specific connotations of activation had been developed. She proposed (Duffy, 1962) a continuum of organismic excitation related both to the existing stimulus situation and certain internal factors which together produce important changes in behaviour. Malmo (1959) has similarly proposed a continuum of activation (low to high) indexed at the one extreme by deep sleep and at the other by what he terms 'excited states'. Neurophysiologically, it is proposed that a position on the continuum is a function of the amount of cortical bombardment by the ascending reticular activating system (A.R.A.S.) such that the greater the cortical bombardment the higher the activation. Such activation effects are relative to the individual.

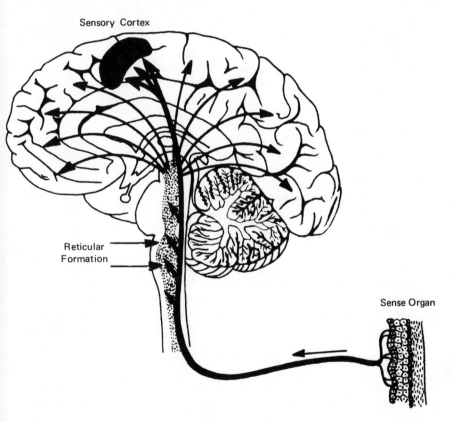

Sensory Cortex

Reticular Formation

Sense Organ

Fig. 5. The Reticular Activating System.

The A.R.A.S. is a nonspecific, diffuse projection system forming a central core in the C.N.S. extending from the medulla of the lower brain stem to the thalamus in the diencephalon (Fig. 5) and shown by Moruzzi and Magoun (1949) to be an arousal system on which the cortex is dependent for its *organised* activity. Its importance in learning and performance is therefore of considerable interest.

Samuels (1959) maintains that the reticular structures play a critical role in the learning process in that their arousal functions provide indispensable facilitation for perception, attention, learning and motor activity.

Fuster (1958) found that concurrent A.R.A.S. stimulation of moderate intensity improved accuracy and speed of visual discrimination reaction and Duffy (1962) suggested that the degree of activation appeared to affect both sensory sensitivity and motor response. Bernhaut et al (1953) stress the importance of movement by maintaining that kinesthetic stimulation is of more importance than visual or auditory stimuli for reticular stimulation. Carpenter (1959) experimenting on rats found that twenty two and one half hours of movement deprivation resulted in greater disruption of behaviour than did the same duration of either sound deprivation or light deprivation. It is also interesting to note that Kulka et al (1960) have proposed that rocking and head banging and other such rhythmic movements seen in infants with prolonged deprivation may be an attempt to gratify their own kinesthetic needs.

In view of these findings and the considerable evidence which is amassing from experimental work on sensory and perceptual deprivation (Newton and Levine, 1968) the notion of the human organism as a passive responder to stimuli is hardly tenable. The reader will be reminded of Gibson's (1968) differentiation between *imposed perception* which occurs when the organs are passive and stimulation impinges on them and *obtained perception* which occurs when the senses are considered as perceptual systems which actively seek information.

Classically—as Hebb (1955) has reported—the input from a display follows a direct sensory route (sensory nerve → sensory tract → sensory nucleus of thalamus → sensory projection areas of the cortex) providing a quick and efficient method of transmitting information. What Moruzzi and Magoun (1949) proposed was a second pathway, diffuse in nature formed by collaterals (neural branches) from the classical ascending afferent pathways projecting onto the reticular activating system (R.A.S.). These workers implanted electrodes in the R.A.S. of cats and discovered that stimulation with a small electrical current had the same awakening effect on a drowsy cat as a scratch on the head. They concluded that stimulation of the R.A.S. 'aroused' the cortex rather than being responsible for the relaying of any specific message. Without such an arousal system, sensory impulses by the direct route reach the sensory cortex but go no further.

Magoun (1963) has suggested a function of the R.A.S. whereby sensory information is either alerted to or screened out according to the significance established for it by previous experience. This is more analogous to the concept of 'attention' proposed by Adams (1966). An everyday illustration of the phenomenon would be the way in which a sleeping mother may be sensitive to her infant's cry where the father in the same room might not be awakened.

Apparently the stimulation which causes arousal is that to which a person has not habituated i.e. stimuli which cause arousal are those which are novel, very intense or signals of danger (all of which habituate less easily). More generally, arousal level is raised by tasks providing a challenge, demanding an effort or providing an incentive (Welford, 1968). In this connection, Melzack (1968) reports the results of experiments on dogs raised in cages that drastically reduce (but do not eliminate) sensory inputs (Melzack, 1954; Thompson and Heron, 1954). The most characteristic feature of dogs which underwent such percpetual deprivation was the extremely high level of arousal that pervaded all their behaviour. Almost anything new in their environment—including a new food pan—raised the level of excited activity.

Stimulation of the cortex by sensory projections from the A.R.A.S. should not be conceived as a one way process. Feedback loops of great complexity are involved. The so-called cortico-reticular loop for example is responsible for arousal messages to the cortex but in turn, the cortex can instruct the A.R.A.S. whether to continue sending arousal messages or else to inhibit such messages.

In addition to its function as an activator of the cortex the A.R.A.S. also has facilitatory or inhibitory effects on the motor outflow. It apparently has regulatory control over all the motor activities of the body and can modify muscular movements of both the voluntary and reflex type. While stimulation of a motor centre by an electrical current will produce the appropriate muscular response, it is jerky and uncontrolled. Such movements are normally aided and refined by other motor centres of the cortex acting through the reticular formation (French, 1957).

One of the earlier findings in the field of 'activation' was an improvement in performance as arousal rose from a low level up to some optimum and then a deterioration in performance with increasing arousal.

An inverted U relation of this nature (Duffy, 1932; Freeman, 1948; Hebb, 1955; and Malmo, 1959) between drive and performance was implied in the Yerkes-Dodson law (revived by Broadhurst, 1959) which briefly proposed that:

> ... an easy discrimination is more easily learned by an animal the higher the motivation but that for more difficult discriminations learning is best at an intermediate level of motivation, the optimum

valve shifting to a lower level as the discrimination becomes harder (Broadbent 1965).

At an everyday level, it will be appreciated that simple repetitive tasks can be performed quite adequately with a background of music but more complex tasks would be affected adversely by such extraneous sources of stimulation. Hockey (1969) in reviewing the effects of noise on task efficiency confirms that some tasks improve with the addition of noise while others deteriorate–the most distinguishing feature being the complexity or difficulty of the task. He suggests it is reasonable to suppose that noise improves performance when arousal is too low for the task and impairs it when arousal is already optimal or too high.

An interpretation of why this relationship should hold is in debate. With regard to the facilitation provided as arousal goes from a low level to some optimal state, both Freeman (1931) and Hebb (1955) have suggested increased activation as possibly rendering cortical cells more susceptible to firing by weak signals than might otherwise be the case. The decline with increased intensity of arousal is explained by Welford (1968). If the stream of impulses impinging on the cortex becomes very intense, the cells are not only rendered more sensitive but are actually fired. This has the effect of making the cortex 'noisy' (in communication theory terms) and resulting in a blurring of signals coming from outside or passing from one point of the brain to another. More recently (Naatenen, 1974) the whole basis of the inverted 'U' relationship has been questioned and it has been suggested that the fall-off in performance after some optimal state has been reached may be an artefact of the experimental methodology used to investigate the relationship.

The activation/arousal dichotomy

It is possible now to look at the differentiation which has been made between autonomic *activation* and cortical *arousal*. A mechanism (A.R.A.S.) has been suggested whereby processes of facilitation and inhibition affect the amount and kind of stimulation that reaches the cortex from the sensory receptors and from the cortex to the muscular systems. Summarising a larger number of recent neurological studies, Samuels (1959) concludes that all sensory modalities–both interoceptive and exteroceptive–give off collaterals to both the brain stem and the thalamic reticular systems. Thus, visual, auditory, olfactory, tactile, pain, proprioceptive and visceral stimuli are all capable of activating the reticular system.

It would appear on this basis, that the visceral brain (comprising the hippocampus, amygdala, cingulum, septum and hypothalamus) which is responsible for the control and *activation* of the autonomic system gives off collaterals to the reticular system in the same way as the ascending afferent pathways. Eysenck (1968) suggests that *activation* of the visceral brain will have an *arousal* effect on the cortex similar to that produced by the A.R.A.S. Cortical arousal in these terms may have two different origins:

1. stimulation via the ascending and descending pathways of the reticular system which do not involve the visceral brain (hence no influence from autonomic activation),
2. stimulation via the ascending and descending pathways of the reticular system which relate to the hypothalamus. This implies both an autonomic (emotional) activation and a cortical arousal.

Thus, as Eysenck suggests *activation* always leads to arousal but *arousal* often comes from stimulation which does not involve activation and in the interests of clarity it is important to differentiate between the two terms. He further equates his personality factor of extraversion/introversion with differential thresholds in the various parts of the A.R.A.S. and the factor of neuroticism with differential thresholds of activation in the visceral brain.

Decision-making

As the skill learner progresses from being a relatively unskilled to a relatively skilled performer, there is a successive refinement both in his information processing abilities (see Section 3) and in his graded response(s). Skilled behaviour which is guided by information from the external environment necessitates an efficient translation between such information and the motor response. Such stimulus-response mapping involves decision-making which is not dependent solely on external information or level of arousal.

The limitations of a strictly mechanistic information theory approach have already been touched on. They are further elaborated by Meredith (1966):

Any day you can witness men exposed to information who make decisions manifestly not necessitated by the information and often, indeed incompatible with it. It is information *selected* and often *transmuted* and further *augmented* from our internal source, which shapes the decision.

While decision theorists look to current information processing for evidence of the variables that control decision-making, it is clear that this alone cannot account for the effect it may produce within the individual.

Available information as Meredith (1966) again points out, is only the starting point of a decision:

> Preference and belief are the other two factors.
> Preference expresses taste and temperament and it influences both the selection of information and the felt relevance of particular beliefs.

Dynamic decision theory attempts to deal with variables in the current situation which affect decision-making as well as those which are due to past experience (Edwards and Tversky, 1967). While therefore the impact of information processing on decision-making assumes a central role in decision theory, it will be appreciated that the *value* of the stimulus—its *utility* value—will influence decision-making as will the *probability* of the outcome of a particular class of event. In addition, different kinds of information may have different utility values for different persons or for the same person on different occasions (Whiting et al, 1974) and such values may affect the strategies adopted. It may become necessary in future research to pay more attention to the *cognitive style* (Witkin et al, 1962) of the learner as Broadbent (1971) has recently intimated.

To summarise the position stated above, what is being suggested, is that the display resonates with energy of many kinds and such energy impinges upon the perceptual systems. It does not become relevant information from the point of view of decision-making until the individual has put an interpretation upon it. This involves the transduction of physical energy to electrical energy (neural coding) at the interface between the external and internal environments; the registration of such energy at the projection and association areas of the cortex and its interpretation on the basis of past experience. These processes involve *selection* from amongst the totality of energy transforms and their interpretation in relation to the existing situation and the individual's past experience. *Selection and interpretation* have highly subjective connotations and it is not surprising to find that in most skill learning and performance experiments, individual differences account for a major proportion of the variance. There are many personal factors which may influence the perception of a situation and hence the resultant decision and motor action.

The concept of selective attention already discussed in some detail, implies a form of decision-making. The decision to focus attention on one area of the display rather than another or to switch from one analyser to another. Meredith (1966) discusses this procedure succintly:

> But we do not need to be told that a 'disposition to attend' is not as a rule a fixed 'state of mind'. Experience in school teaches everyone that an *effort* to attend is usually needed and that attention fluctuates. And

since 'attention' by its very meaning connotes a selection from the totality of incoming stimulation, as contrasted with a diffuse awareness of being alive there must at some moment for such change of attention be a decision to select this stimulus rather than that.

It would appear therefore that incorporation of decision theory findings into an information processing model permits a more meaningful and quantifiable approach to skill learning and performance. It also enables the concept of errors to be handled successfully—a problem of which information theory takes no account. Such errors are clearly not random.

Perhaps it is not surprising to the layman that personal characteristics affect decision-making. Nevertheless, in relation to experimental psychology, Eysenck (1966) has recently found a need to stress the effects that individual differences have on the performance of any skill and to suggest that such effects are often ignored. In terms of individual differences and cognitive style, Broadbent (1958) raises the interesting possibility of there being categories (or a continuum) of information samplers which might be suitably termed 'long-term samplers' and 'short-term samplers' which characterises their decision-making strategies. This does not necessarily imply that because people take a longer period of time to make their responses that they necessarily require more time in which to sample information. It is conceivable for example that the delay occurs in the decision-making itself which is based on a *similar* quantity of information. Such a conception relates to problems of speed-accuracy trade-off (Eysenck, 1968; Whiting and Hutt, 1972).

Presumably, with *perfect* knowledge—if this is a meaningful concept— perfect decisions would be made. The fact that decisions are very often imperfect or temporary expedients reflects the fact that most decisions are based on imperfect knowledge and under such conditions the decision-maker is taking a risk. The nature of the risk has to be estimated on the basis of the outcome if a wrong decision is made. A similar concept is of course fundamental to inferential statistics and the notion of significance. Over attention to arbitrary levels of significance misses the point that every statistical significance level reported in these terms ($p < .05$; $p < .01$ etc.) indicates the risk that would be taken in utilising the results of a particular experiment. As Mowrer (1960) points out:

> Statistical procedures cannot 'tell us what do do'. That doing presupposes deciding and that deciding is contingent not only upon the available evidence but also upon the nature of the risks or values which are involved.

The necessity of making decisions on the basis of imperfect knowledge, may be reflected either in the fact that perfect knowledge is not available, or that *time* or *past experience* does not permit the abstraction of such information. Economy of time is presumably a factor of efficient decision-makers in skill learning and performance situations and is reflected in their ability to quickly amass the necessary information to deal with the demands of the situation. It is helpful to think of a time-continuum in relation to decision-making. At one extreme, the time limits may be so short that decisions have to be made on the basis of limited information. This is reflected very often in talk about life and death decisions and is a feature of traffic accidents which occur every day. All too often, a wrong decision is made, often on the basis of inadequate information under the existing time constraints or because the display was so confused as to prevent the abstraction of the relevant information. At the other end of the time continuum, a decision may not be required for a period of months or even years and information can be amassed and assessed over this time. While it does not necessarily follow that the right decision will be made after such a long period of assembling the evidence, it does make it more likely.

Performance in fast ball games is a good example of decision-making on the basis of short-time sampling. As Poulton (1965) has pointed out, in hitting a moving ball, three reasonably precise predictions are necessary:

1   The correct stroke to use—which may or may not be a ballistic action.
2   Where to pass the ball after it has been acquired.
3   The correct timing in order to hit the ball with the right amount of power when it is in the correct place. This involves predicting, when the ball will be in the correct place for hitting, when to initiate the stroke to reach the ball at that time and the effort to be applied to the stroke.

All this information must be computed in a fraction of a second and adaptive decisions made. (Those who underestimate the magnitude of this feat on the part of the human brain should consider the problems faced by the late Paul Fitts (1964) in attempting to programme a computer to hit a baseball bowled by a top-class pitcher!). Under such conditions, it is not surprising that a reasonably quick reaction time is necessary in addition to prolonged experience within a game in order to be able to assess the situation in such a brief interval of time and make decisions of this nature. In this respect, it is interesting to note Meredith's (1966) contention that if consciousness is a necessary condition for decision-making, it does not follow that the process itself is something of which we are aware. The experienced player is often unaware of what influences his decision—he is at the 'autonomous' level of performance (Fitts and Posner, 1966). He 'knows' what to do and when to do it, but it would appear that he is often not conscious of having made a decision. In relation to the proposed time-continuum for decision-making, it would seem to be good advice in any situation to:

> ... formulate our strategy not by reference to some arbitrary minimum time-factor but by reference to the time available. (Meredith, 1966)

If in a games playing situation for example, a player is able to wait for a longer period of time before making a decision (because he has a fast reaction time or because being experienced in such situations he can read the display efficiently) he can allow for unpredictable events and thus behave more adaptively. To commit himself too soon can be as disastrous as committing himself too late. There is also the additional advantage that the longer he delays his movements, the less time available to his opponent for detection and analysis.

To Meredith (1966), decision-making is often a geometrical event. A cutting away, a removal of unwanted stimulation from the focus of attention. In Rabbitt's (1967) terms, one must learn what information is irrelevant as well as that which *is* relevant.

The geometrical nature of such decision-making is evidenced in the chess player or team player in a competitive situation:

> He is able to compete not merely by reason of his capacity for putting strategy against strategy, but by his interpretative skill in grasping the significance of the pattern of relations of men on the board (or field). (Meredith, 1966)

Output Characteristics

The main part of the work discussed so far has related to the input characteristics of the proposed model and though mention has been made in passing of the linkage with efferent output this has not been developed. It is not intended to develop the output characteristics to any extent at this stage since they merit a book in themselves. However, it is fitting that this overview should establish the important concepts which can be followed up by the reader in other sources. For this reason a brief attempt is made to put output characteristics into some perspective.

In general, the point has been raised (page 6) that knowledge of results is essential for the development of skilled behaviour. Such feedback information may be (and usually is) multichannelled. But this may not be the case in so-called *ballistic** movements which may be pre-programmed in their entirety (although such programmes may be established with the aid of feedback). It might be asked therefore how such movements are set up in the first place? Whether refined ballistic movements (particularly those involving effort control) have developed from other more gross and less-refined ballistic movements? In a similar way, it might be asked whether movements initially carried out under feedback control, gradually come to be programmed (autonomous) to a greater and greater extent.

In relation to 'open' skills, it has been pointed out that for successful performances, it is necessary to fit the response (often ballistic in nature) to the appropriate information from the environment. This is an important aspect of 'timing'. 'Timing' can also be looked upon in terms of the duration of a movement or the duration of movement might be utilised as a timing device.

Now, just as the skill performer has to learn to attend to information from the environment which has a steering function, so it would appear, he has to learn to select on the output side. It has been suggested that the sequential input of information is of some importance and in a similar way, sequential output not only in spatial terms but in temporal terms is also important. The appropriate muscle groups must be selected (not necessarily at a conscious level) and their sequential order of firing arranged and timed to fit the existing situation. In this respect, Provins (1967) comments:

> There is evidence to suggest that in infancy and for many years afterwards, a child spends a good deal of his time in learning to discriminate the muscles involved in bringing about a given type of movement and that the same thing happens in a novice learning a new motor skill (Bair, 1901; Landerwold, 1946).
> Such discrimination as Basmajian (1963) has recently shown, may involve discrete motor units, but once discriminated, the appropriate units still have to be selected for any given situation. It may be hypothesised that this selection procedure takes time, depending upon the range of possible alternatives, in much the same way that the time for identification of a stimulus appears to depend on the size of the stimulus set or ensemble.

The importance of kinesthetic information in the control of motor output is well documented. What is less clear, is its necessity for learning and performance and under what conditions. Some support for kinesthetic control comes from the following kinds of study:

---

*In psychological terms such movements are pre-programmed as a whole and cannot be influenced by current information monitoring, (Vince, 1948).

1 Lesions of the CNS

For example, lesions in dorsal roots and dorsal ganglions result in ataxia or inco-ordination of movement (Chase, 1965)

Patients who cannot hear, show impaired control of speech. Similarly, lesions involving peripheral sensory input channels can functionally result in profound motor deficits.

2 Delayed feedback

For example, delayed auditory feedback results in:

(a) increase in mean sound pressure level
(b) slurring of speech
(c) decreased rate
(d) repetition errors

Smith and Smith (1962) report similar findings for delayed visual feedback.

3 Reafference experiments of for example Held and Hein (1963).

In all these cases, it is being assumed that the nervous system is being deprived of information essential for normal motor output. If sensory feedback has such a vital part to play, does it have equal importance at various stages of skill learning? It is difficult to be dogmatic in this respect. What would appear to happen, is that in the early stages of acquiring a skill, frequent sampling is necessary because of the large output errors which normally occur. There is then a progressively reduced sampling of such information as more successive refinements of the programming take place and error correction becomes less necessary. Some highly learned motor sequences probably operate essentially independent of sensory feedback. In terms of control system theory, the suggestion is made that learning might involve the progressive change from closed loop control to open loop control, via progressive improvement in the central programming of motor command patterns. It is also worth considering at this stage the concept of the monitoring of efferent impulses. Referring back to previous comments about feedback control it will be recalled that an error-correction system is proposed operating on information about the departure of the output of the system from some predetermined end state which results from the matching operations of the error detection systems. An appropriate pattern of motor command is then programmed which results in a change in motor output designed to correct for the error previously detected (Chase, 1965).

The idea that the human system might make use of efferent information (i.e. the monitoring of motor outflow) is not a new one. Such speculations were made for example by Helmholz (1925) and James (1890). The implication here is that the skill performer is able in some way to monitor the information which is given to the effectors and to make use of this information in making ongoing behaviour adaptive. Festinger and Kirkpatrick-Canon (1965) summarise the position:

If in the central nervous system outgoing motor nerve impulses are monitored and recorded, then information would also exist concerning spatial efferent impulses, that is a record of the specific directions given to the musculature.

The general model concerned, postulates simultaneous activation of the pattern of neural activity which will be translated into a motor command pattern and the pattern of neural activity which will be used as a standard for monitoring control of the motor output.

References

ADAMS, J.A. (1966). Mechanisms of motor responding. In E.A. Bilodeau (Ed.) *Acquisition of Skill.* New York: Academic Press.

ARGYLE, M. & KENDON, A. (1967). The experimental analysis of social performance. In L. Berkowitz (Ed.) *Advances in Experimental Social Psychology, Vol. 3.* New York: Academic Press.

AVERBACH, E. & SPERLING, A. (1960). Short-term storage of information in vision. In C. Cherry (Ed.) *Information Theory.* London: Butterworth.

BARTLETT, F. (1958). *Thinking: an experimental and social study.* London: Allen & Unwin.

BERNHAUT, M., GELLHORN, E. & RASMUSSEN, A.T. (1953) Experimental contributions to problems of consciousness. *J. Neurophysiol.,* **16**, 21-35.

BROADBENT, D.E. (1958). *Perception and Communication.* London: Pergamon.

BROADBENT, D.E. (1965). Applications of information theory and decision theory to human performance and reaction. In N. Wiener and J.P. Schade (Eds.) *Progress in Brain Research.* Amsterdam: Elsevier.

BROADBENT, D.E. (1971). *Decision and Stress.* London: Academic Press.

BROADHURST, P.L. (1959). The interaction of task difficulty and motivation. The Yerkes-Dodson law revived. *Acta Psychologica,* **16**, 321-328.

CARPENTER, P.B. (1959). The effects of sensory deprivation on behaviour in the white rat. Doctoral dissertation, Florida State University.

CHASE, I. (1965). An information flow model of the organisation of human activity. Parts I and II. *J. Nerv. Ment. Dis.,* **140**, 239-251.

CHERRY, E.C. (1957). Some experiments on the recognition of speech with one and two ears. *J. Acoust. Soc. Amer.*, **25**, 975-979.

CHERRY, E.C. (1960). *Information Theory.* London: Butterworth.

CROSSMAN, E.R.F.W. (1966). Information processes in human skill. *Brit. Med. Bull.*, **20**, 32-37.

DEUTSCH, J.A. & DEUTSCH, D. (1963). Attention: some theoretical considerations. *Psychol. Rev.*, **70**, 80-90.

DUFFY, E. (1932). The measurement of muscular tension as a technique for the study of emotional tendencies. *Am. J. Psychol.*, **44**, 146-162.

DUFFY, E. (1951). The concept of energy mobilisation. *Psychol. Rev.*, **5**, 30-40.

DUFFY, E. (1962). *Activation and Behaviour.* New York: Wiley.

EDWARDS, W. & TVERSKY, A. (1967). *Decision-making.* Harmondsworth: Penguin.

ELKIND, D. & WEISS, J. (1967). Studies in perceptual development. III. Perceptual exploration. *Child Dev.*, **19**, 1-28.

EYSENCK, H.J. (1966). Personality and experimental psychology. *Bull. Brit. Psychol. Soc.*, **19**, 1-28.

EYSENCK, H.J. (1968). *Biological Basis of Personality.* Springfield: Thomas.

FESTINGER, L. & KIRKPATRICK-CANON, L. (1965). Information about spatial location based on knowledge about efference. *Psychol. Rev.*, **72**, 373-384.

FITTS, P.M. (1964). Perceptual-motor skill learning. In A.W. Melton (Ed.) *Categories of Human Learning.* London: Academic Press.

FITTS, P.M. & POSNER, M.I. (1967). *Human Performance.* Belmont: Brooks/Cole.

FREEMAN, C.L. (1931). The galvanic phenomenon and conditioned responses. *J. Genet. Psychol.*, **3**, 529-539.

FREEMAN, C.L. (1948). *The Energetics of Human Behaviour.* New York: Cornell University Press.

FRENCH, J.D. (1957). The reticular formation, *Scientific Amer.*, May.

FUSTER, J.M. (1958). Effects of stimulation of the brain stem on tachistoscopic perception. *Science*, **127**, 150.

GIBSON, J.J. (1968). *The Senses Considered as Perceptual Systems.* London: Allen & Unwin.

GUTHRIE, E.R. (1952). *The Psychology of Learning.* New York: Harper and Row.

HEBB, D.O. (1955). Drives and the C.N.S. *Psychol. Rev.*, **62**, 243-254

HELD, R. & HEIN, A. (1963). A movement produced stimulation in the development of visually guided behaviour. *J. Comp. Physiol. Psychol.*, **56**, 872-874.

HELMHOLZ, H. Von. (1925). *Treatise on Physiological Optics, Vols. 2 & 3.* New York: Optical Society of America.

HOCKEY, R. (1969). Noise and efficiency. *New Scientist,* 42, 244-246.

HORN, G. (1965). Physiological and psychological aspects of selective perception. In D.S. Lehrman, R.A. Hinde, & E. Shaw (Eds.) *Advances in the Study of Behaviour.* Vol. 1. New York: Wiley.

JAMES, W. (1890). *The Principles of Psychology.* New York: Holt.

KNAPP, B.N. (1964). *Skill in Sport.* London: Routledge & Kegan Paul.

KULKA, A., FRY, C., & GOLDSTEIN, F.J. (1960). Kinesthetic needs in infancy. *Am. J. Orthopsychiat.,* 30, 306-314.

LIVINGSTON, R.B. (1959). Central control of receptors and sensory transmission systems. In J. Field (Ed.) *Handbook of Physiology, Vol. 2.* Bethesda: American Physiological Society.

LORENZ, K. (1937). *Studies in Animal Behaviour, I.* London: Methuen.

MAGOUN, H.W. (1963). *The Waking Brain.* Springfield: Thomas.

MALMO, R.B. (1959). Activation—a neurophysiological dimension. *Psychol. Rev.,* 66, 367-386.

MARLER, P. (1961). The filtering of external stimuli during instinctive behaviour. In W.H. Thorpe & O. Zangwill (Eds.) *Current Problems in Animal Behaviour.* London: Cambridge University Press.

MELZACK, R. (1954). The genesis of emotional behaviour: an experimental study of the dog. *J. Comp. Physiol. Psychol.,* 47, 166-168.

MELZACK, R. (1968). A neuropsychological approach to heredity-environment. In G. Newton & S. Levine (Eds.) *Early Experience and Behaviour.* Springfield: Thomas.

MEREDITH, G.P. (1966). *Instruments of Communication.* London: Pergamon.

MILLER, G.A., GALANTER, E. & PRIBRAM, K.H. (1960). *Plans and the Structure of Behaviour.* New York: Holt, Rinehart and Winston.

MORAY, N. (1969). *Attention: selective processes in vision and hearing.* London: Hutchinson.

MORUZZI, A. & MAGOUN, H.W. (1949). Brain stem reticular formation and activation of the E.E.G. *Electroenceph. Clin. Neurophysiol.,* 1, 455-473.

MOWRER, O.H. (1960). *Learning Theory and the Symbolic Process.* New York: Wiley.

NAATENEN, R. (1974). The inverted-U relationship between activation and performance: a critical review. In S. Kornblum (Ed.) *Attention and Performance IV.* New York: Academic Press.

NEWTON, G. & LEVINE, S. (Eds.) (1968). *Early Experience and Behaviour.* Springfield: Thomas.

NORMAN, D.A. (1969). *Memory and Attention: an introduction to human information processing.* New York: Wiley.

POULTON, E.C. (1957). On prediction in skilled movements. *Psychol. Bull.,* 54, 467-478.

POULTON, E.C. (1965). Skill in fast ball games. *Biol. & Human Affairs,* **31**, 1-5.

POSNER, M.I. & KLEIN, R.M. (1974). On the functions of consciousness. In S. Kornblum (Ed.) *Attention and Performance IV.* New York: Academic Press.

PRIBRAM, K.H. (1966). Some dimensions of remembering. Steps toward a neuropsychological theory of remembering. In J. Gaito (Ed.) *Macromolecules and Behaviour.* London: Academic Press.

PROVINS, K. (1967). Some recent advances in the study of motor skills. Report of the sixth national conference in physical education. Adelaide: Australian Physical Education Association.

RABBITT, P.M. (1967). Learning to ignore irrelevant information. *Am. J. Psychol.,* **80**, 1-13.

RENSHAW, P. (1974). The nature of human movement studies and its relationship with physical education. Conference report of the Association of Principals of Women's Colleges of Physical Education.

SAMUELS, I. (1959). Reticular mechanisms and behaviour. *Psychol. Bull.,* **56**, 1-25.

SKINNER, B.F. (1961). *Cumulative Record.* New York: Appleton-Century-Crofts.

SMITH, K.U. & SMITH, W.M. (1962). *Perception and Motion.* Philadelphia: Saunders.

STOUT, G.F. (1899). *Manual of Psychology.* London: University Correspondence College.

THOMPSON, W.R. & HERON, W. (1954). Exploratory behaviour in normal and restricted dogs. *J. Comp. Physiol. Psychol.,* **47**, 77-82.

THORPE, W.H. (1964). *Learning and Instinct in Animals.* Cambridge Mass.: Harvard University Press.

TINBERGEN, N. (1942). An objective study of the innate behaviour of animals. *Bibliotheca Biotheoretica I,* Rijkuniversiteit te Leiden.

TITCHENER, E.B. (1901). *Experimental Psychology I. Student's Manual.* London: Macmillan.

TREISMAN, A.M. (1966). Our limited attention. *Adv. Science,* **22**, 600-611.

TREISMAN, A.M. & GEFFEN, G. (1967). Selective attention: perception or response? *Quart. J. Exp. Psychol.,* **19**, 1-17.

VAN OLST, E.H. ORLEBEKE, J.F. & FOKKEMA, S.O. (1967). Skin conductance as a measure of tonic and phasic arousal. In A.F. Sanders (Ed.) *Attention and Performance.* Amsterdam: North Holland Publishing Co.,

VERNON, M.D. (1962). *The Psychology of Perception.* Harmondsworth: Penguin.

VINCE, M.A. (1948). Corrective movements in a pursuit task. *Quart. J. Exp. Psychol.,* **1**, 85-103.

WELFORD, A.T. (1968). *Fundamentals of Skill.* London: Methuen.

WHITING, H.T.A. (1969). *Acquiring Ball Skill: a psychological interpretation.* London: Bell.

WHITING, H.T.A. (1972). Theoretical models for an understanding of perceptual-motor skill performance. *Quest,* **17**, 24-34.

WHITING, H.T.A. & HUTT, J.W.R. (1972). The effects of personality and ability on speed of decision regarding the directional aspects of ball flight. *J. Motor Behav.,* **4**, 89-98.

WHITING, H.T.A., HARDMAN, K.H., HENDRY, L.B. & JONES, M.G. (1974). *Personality and Performance in Physical Education and Sport.* London: Kimpton.

WHITING, H.T.A. & COCKERILL, I.M. (1972). The development of a simple ballistic skill with and without visual control. *J. Motor Behav.,* **4**, 155-162.

WILKINSON, R.T. (1967). Evoked response and reaction time. In A.F. Sanders (Ed.) *Attention and Performance.* Amsterdam: North Holland Publishing Co.

WITKIN, H.A., DYK, R.B., FATERSON, D.R. & KARP, S.A. (1962). *Psychological Differentiation:* New York: Wiley.

WOODWORTH, R.S. & SCHLOSBERG, H. (1954). *Experimental Psychology.* New York: Holt.

2

MOVEMENT AND ITS OUTCOME

Section

2 MOVEMENT AND ITS OUTCOME

The possible confusion between *movement* and its *outcome* was raised in Section 1 (page 5). In view of the important implications of such a dichotomy, the concept is elaborated in this Section from a number of different viewpoints.

In one of the most oft-quoted definitions of skill, Knapp (1964) extrapolating from the work of Guthrie (1952) talks about:

> ... the learned ability to bring about predetermined results with maximum certainty often with the minimum outlay of time or energy or both.

Skill or *ability* in this sense, is judged by the degree of success in bringing about a predetermined result and as such is a relative term. We do not observe skill directly but infer its presence by the achievements of the person. A concept of this nature that does not *directly* refer to behaviour but that is nevertheless closely tied to it, is known in the psychological literature as an *intervening variable*. The distinction is put in another helpful way by the philosopher Ryle (1969) in suggesting that *skill* is not an act, but a disposition, the power to act. What are observable and can be evaluated are *movements* and the *outcome of such movements*. (N.B. the dichotomy)—i.e. means and ends.

Thus, we may have *skill* in relation to the performance of a number of different *skills* where the latter may be defined in terms of predetermined outcomes or results.

To summarise, I am saying that a person who exhibits competence in carrying out tasks which can be clearly defined in terms of their required end result is a skilled person and possesses skill in achieving that particular goal. This is the result of learning and as was suggested in Section 1, one of the criteria which differentiates the kind of complex behaviour which it is wished to designate as *skilled*, from other complex forms of behaviour such as 'fixed

37

action patterns' in animals is the time course of the learning process. Progress along the continuum from unskilled to skilled generally involves a *protracted* period of learning.

Thus, my present emphasis is on the evaluation of *skill* and not skills. That is not to say that evaluation of *skill*s might not be a useful procedure. Very often for example it is necessary to be concerned with the criteria for selection of particular skills in relation to curriculum building and with discussions about which skills to teach to particular age groups. What I shall attempt to do instead is to elaborate upon some relatively straightforward concepts in evaluation but which I consider to be important. You will note therefore in relation to what I say later the *subjectivity* in my selection.

Skill then is an intervening variable—covert and therefore not *directly* capable of evaluation by the techniques currently available to us. We normally claim to assess a person's skill level in solving a particular motor problem arising out of the external environment, either *directly* by observing his movements or more indirectly by observing the outcome of such movements. I shall want to spend some time in differentiating therefore between *movement* and its *outcome* and also on the relationship between learning and performance.

The simple difference I am emphasising can be illustrated by writing on the blackboard. The observable movements are to be distinguished from the chalkmarks on the blackboard which are the outcome of such movements. A dichotomy of this kind reflects back upon my definition of *a skill* as a pre-determined end result. The difficulty in being precise in this respect is apparent from an examination of those complex activities found in sport of all kinds. In the activity of golf for example there are many skills with well-defined end results (e.g. putting the ball into the hole from a position on the green). There are other behavioural acts which are carried out in an attempt to achieve some end result which is less clearly defined—such as driving the ball up the fairway onto the green when it is known that the intention is not to 'hole' the ball but to get it to come to rest in as *favourable a position as possible*. Again, for example, in the activity of high-jumping, the end result may ultimately be to jump *as high as possible*. Sub-goals consist of jumping the heights to which the bar is set. A number of different movement patterns may enable a performer to achieve such sub-goals (e.g. Western roll, Eastern cut-off, Fosbury Flop). Such styles/techniques can be classified as skills, in which case, the end-result is clearly different from those skills which can be defined independently of the movement. They are certainly examples of complex learned behaviour intentionally carried out, but the end result is conformity to a movement pattern generally prescribed by a teacher or a coach. Thus, in jumping a predetermined height, the concern is more with the external criterion than with the movement pattern adopted (although there may be a correlation between the two). On the other hand, in performing a *Western* roll for example, the concern is with reproducing a prescribed movement pattern and success is judged not by the ability to jump a certain height, but by the ability to reproduce a relatively constrained movement pattern which because of individual differences in interpretation and physique cannot be absolutely defined. It is the performer's interpretation of a model that has been prescribed for him by demonstration, verbal mediation, film techniques etc. One of the major difficulties facing the teacher of such skills is that of establishing for the learner an adequate model against which he may discriminate his own attempts. Furthermore, the success of the learner's attempts is subjectively assessed by the teacher in relation to the model which *he* has in mind. Thus the *skill* of the teacher both in establishing such a model and in being able to 'compare' such a model with the attempts made by the learner and provide adequate feedback which may aid such learning at various stages of development is continually called into question. Interestingly enough, the skill of the teacher is not usually evaluated in these terms, but in terms of the success of the people he is teaching i.e. in terms of *their* outcomes and not *his* performance.

As suggested in Section 1 it would appear that the predetermined end result by which specific skills are defined may be:

(a) independent of the way in which it is achieved (in the sense of a definitive movement pattern)
(b) solely in terms of a prescribed movement pattern
(c) a combination of both crieteria.

In terms of evaluation, a confusion of (a) and (b), can sometimes be unfortunate when for example in the performance of skills for which category (a) is appropriate, teachers have laid undue emphasis on conformity to prescribed movement patterns notwithstanding that in many instances (games skills for example) the unconventional performer may have an advantage in that he not only confuses the display for the opposition but he has more opportunity to play against conventional opposition than the latter has to play against unconventional.

In most games skills, it is the outcome which is important (the goal scored, the opponent tackled, the defensive block etc.) not some prescribed movement patterns although the rules of such games may impose constraints on the latter. As Best (1974) illustrates:

> If we were to ask a hockey player, on the eve of an important match, 'which would you prefer, to score three goals in a clumsy manner, or to miss them all with graceful movements?', there is little doubt what the answer would be, at least in most cases!

Learning theory provides interesting illustrations from a completely different frame of reference. Gregory (1970) reminds us of early experiments in maze learning which confirmed the fact that rats can swim a flooded maze after learning to run it dry, thus confirming that it is *not* primarily patterns of movements which are learned. In Tolman's terms, the animals formed 'cognitive maps' which could be negotiated by a variety of means once having been established.

Reflection for a moment will confirm that for example in learning to play squash, improvement comes not so much from being taught new *movements*, as being made aware of possibilities—social facilitation. The possible range of movements to exploit such possibilities are numerous.

In a similar way, Best (1974) confirms that there is another category of sports:

> . . . in each of which the aim cannot be specified in isolation from the aesthetic, for example trampolining, gymnastics, figure-skating and diving. . . There is an intrinsic end, one which cannot be identified independently of the means. . . It is not incidental, but central to those sports *how* one performs the appropriate movements.

To return in the present context to a perhaps more relevant example, in our last Sports Psychology conference (1973) in England an amateur fencing coach (Hammond, 1975) was particularly critical of what had been up to some ten years ago the traditional approach to coaching whereby undue emphasis was placed on conformity to a particular postural and movement style often at the expense of winning! If fencing was in fact one of the performing arts, the criterion adopted might have been appropriate. In as far as it is a competitive sport in which the outcome—hitting one's opponent is the sole criterion of success the older traditional coaching methods were at least open to question.

The psychologist Wright (1967)* enlightens the topic:

> When the troopers of the Heavy Brigade charged the Russian cavalry at Balalava, they had some difficulty in exchanging blows with them since they were unprepared for the Russians' less orthodox approach to mounted swordplay. The Heavy Brigade had been rigidly trained in their sword exercises and had been taught that each cut (specified by a number) had to be followed by a guard. After the engagement, a surgeon was treating a trooper for a sword wound in his scalp and asked how he came by it.

---

*I am obliged to Bill Hammond for bringing this excellent example to my notice.

"Well, I had just cut five (a body cut)", the man replied indignantly, "and the damned fool never guarded at all, but hit me over the head!"

It would appear that in many activities there is and should be less concern or attention to the movement than to its outcome. The philosopher Ricoeur (1966) puts it this way:

> We need to correct radically the opinion that, the 'object' of action, the terminus of 'realisation' is movement. The motive form is not yet the true object of action. Actually, when I act I am not concerned with my body. I say rather that the action 'traverses' my body. . . I am concerned less with my body than with the product of the action: the hanged picture, the strike of the hammer on the head of the nail.

Bernstein (1967) also makes the point that 'n' successive gestures by the same subject are made through 'n' non-coincident trajectories which only gather, as at a focus, in the vicinity of the same required point which is being indicated.

Even in a spatially restricted and ballistic-type skill like hand-cranking in which input and perceptual uncertainty are minimal and which thus depends for its execution largely upon the effector organisation of the operator, Glencross (1973) found that while both fast and slow subjects have significantly common patterns of movement, considerable individual differences are apparent. He comments:

> It is clear that even in such a simple task as hand-cranking, the same end result can be achieved in a variety of ways. Analysis of the film record revealed that the subject used a variety of synergistic postural adjustments.

Bernstein (1967) can perhaps be allowed to make the final comment on this point:

> It follows that the kinematic motor composition of an act is by no means a universal invariant which guarantees the success of the action to be fulfilled. If we turn from the simplest and most repetitive actions to more complex purposeful movements which are frequently multiphasic and conditioned by the need to overcome variable external conditions and resistances such broad variation in the motor composition of movements becomes a universal rule.

From an evaluation point of view, it is worth asking whether or not attention to the movement itself in skill acquisition is desirable? Whether such direction of attention, changes either as one becomes more skilful or whether it is characteristic of particular developmental stages? Unfortunately, research literature in this area is limited, but the few studies I am going to quote indicate the lines along which such enquiries might proceed.

The Russian worker Neverovich (1958) for example was able to show that the efficiency with which tool operations were mastered and the actual standard of their execution were considerably higher when orientation to the method of performing the movement could be produced in the child in the course of training. Instead of the child's attention being directed towards the end product—which was their natural inclination (i.e. getting a nail into a piece of wood), it was directed towards the movement itself by getting them to hammer on a table where no clear-cut end result was involved.

An interesting study was carried out by Manahan (1972) concerned with the formulation of the motor plan in an archery task. In this work, seventh grade female students were divided into two groups. The experimental group were given specific instructions as to the movements they were to use while the control group were allowed to use 'discovery' methods. The experimental group were not only superior on the task set, but were also superior on transfer to a second related task. Now, it should be noted that archery in Knapp's (1964) terms is very much towards the 'closed' end of an 'open closed' skill continuum. An obvious question therefore is whether such procedures would be equally efficacious in skills towards the 'open' end of the continuum. It should also be noted in Manahan's experiment that numbers were small ($N = 16$) and although the two groups were randomly assigned, it is not clear whether they were matched in performance. In addition, it would have been interesting to know what the long-term effects were on performance.

A possible differentiation between 'open' and 'closed' skills in terms of either a varied or constrained movement pattern is of interest and to some extent can throw light on whether or not there are such things as 'open' skills or whether as I have previously suggested it might be better to think of 'closed' skills in *open* situations. (This problem is discussed in detail below.) Some doubt on my own suggestion is cast by recent work of Higgins and Spaeth (1972). These workers make the point that the ability to produce a particular 'ideal' pattern of movement is of importance only insofar as it leads to consistent goal-attainment. The open-skill performer will therefore develop not a single consistent movement pattern but rather a repertoire of movement patterns to match the particular assortment of environmental conditions under which he must perform. They state:

> If indeed successful open skill performance requires diversified movement, then traditional attempts to consistently exhibit a single 'ideal' movement pattern are not only erroneous but detrimental to open-skill

performance. An imposed movement form is of value only if the goal of the activity is to move in a particular way.

In their experimental work, they looked at photographic performances over time of subjects required to perform a dart-throwing task in an 'open' and in a 'closed' skill situation. They were able to show that in an 'open' skill requirement there was a move towards a diversity of patterns of movement matched to environmental conditions while in the 'closed' skill requirement, a move towards consistency in the patterning of movement. Whilst not running directly contrary to the views of Higgins and Spaeth, experiments at present being carried out in my own laboratory (Tyldesley, 1975) would suggest that generation of single, consistent movement patterns in response to given environmental conditions may perhaps not be 'erroneous' and are certainly not 'detrimental' at *all levels* of skilled performance. Further, 'imposed' movement forms are of more widespread value than merely the situation in which the movement is the sole desired end-product. Continued, repetitive practice is essential in the laying down of one consistent motor program, even though a diversity of such movements must be built up to a similar level.

High-speed cinematographical analysis of international table tennis players carrying out similar shots in response to both constant and varied ball trajectories indicated a high intra-subject consistency of movement timing in the expert performer. This high consistency was not eliminated under stressful (game) conditions, rather the temporal constants involved became altered.

The experts appeared to possess well-developed motor programs for each individual shot (consistent to ± 4 msec.) which were initiated earlier in the sequence of play than those of the beginners. The consistency remained across shots of differing spatial tolerance bands, leading to a higher rate of successful bat/ball contact in shots where ball flight at contact was more normal to the plane of the bat. In this way, a shot with a wide tolerance band, e.g. a forehand drive, if produced consistently, would introduce output variability as a function of the inconsistency of the ball onto the bat. This has obvious implications for opponent deception.

Novices typified by a lower ball contact and target contact success rate, indicated poorly developed variable, ballistic actions, initiated later in the train of ball flight events. In view of this, the work of Higgins and Spaeth should perhaps be modified to suggest that whilst the expert's repertoire must be broad to match the assortment of input situations, once the pattern is decided upon, consistency in its performance is a decided advantage. Indeed, the expert will be typified by a wide diversity of movement patterns, but a low intra-response variability of temporal organisation. Were the expert not able to judge, from past experience, the critical timespan of his ballistic actions, then any accuracy in the initiation point of the executive motor program would be functionless.

In concluding this discussion on movement and its outcome, it is worth noting Seashore's (1951) work methods' hypothesis:

> ... which suggests that manipulative skills are acquired by a somewhat haphazard trial-and-error process in such a way that the first fairly successful methods of say, fastening a button, will become established in the learner's repertoire, other methods might exist which are faster and more reliable or involve less effort, but any given individual will have acquired some good and some less good methods.

Should we go along with the child's 'natural' movement methods or should we tell him that he is 'wrong' and in so dong, what evaluative procedures would we utilise in coming to such a conclusion? After all many handicapped people become highly proficient at certain skills, sometimes more able than the non-handicapped.

These characteristic ways of performing alluded to by Seashore, tend to be maintained not only in individual skills, but across wide ranges of skills attempted by the individual in such a way that they come to represent a 'style' of performance peculiar to that individual and we may truly talk about perceptual styles, performance styles, learning styles, teaching styles etc. The evaluation of such 'styles' becomes an important consideration not only in relation to competitive performances but in everyday social interaction situations. The skilful use of such an evaluation can be an important adjunct to the professional psychologist, teacher and medical profession. Perceptual styles have in fact been usefully discussed by Jones (1972) in relation to competitive ball games. Broadbent (1971) suggests that this area of research will be one of the most widely developing over the next decade.

Open-closed skill continuum*

Up to this point, we have operated by using the 'open-closed' skill continuum proposed by Knapp (1964) and it is now necessary to examine the concept in more detail. It will be recalled, that Knapp (1961) extrapolating from the work of Poulton (1950; 1951) put forward the view that:

> ... there is a continuum from skills which are predominantly habitual through to skills which are predominantly perceptual.

---

*I am grateful to my student Robin Russell for some of the ideas presented here.

Since that time, many people have been concerned to place sports skills (in particular) at various points on such a continuum with field games being towards the 'open' end and throwing events in athletics towards the 'closed' end. As I commented in Section 1, critique can be made of this approach since many of the sub-skills involved in field games are ballistic in nature i.e. in the psychological sense (since their execution occupies such little time), information from the environment can have no steering function. I feel there have been some misconceptions which are less apparent in Poulton's (1950) earlier analysis. He proposed a continuum which depended upon the *predictability* of environmental signs. Thus, an 'open' skill to Poulton (1950) was:

> ... a skill in which the relevant environmental signals can rarely be predicted accurately in advance.

and a *closed* skill was:

> ... a practised skill in which the relevant environmental signals can be predicted accurately in advance.

The whole problem centres around the word 'prediction' and as Poulton (1950) states:

> ... there can be no such thing as an 'unpractised closed skill', for a skill cannot become closed until it has been practised sufficiently often for all the relevant environmental signals to be predictable. An unpractised but potentially closed skill is still to this extent an 'open' skill.

We must remind ourselves, that predictability in the psychological sense, is essentially personal, it implies being wise after the event. Similar difficulties have arisen when *redundancy* is defined independently of the person processing the information. What is redundant for one person is not redundant for another. Thus, even if such an 'open-closed' skill continuum is a useful one, positioning a particular skill on such a continuum can only be done *relative to the person performing the skill.* Shifts along the continuum from person to person and from occasion to occasion for particular skills are to be expected.

Not only must the usefulness of such a continuum be questioned, but also the contention that so called 'closed' skills are mainly habitual whereas 'open' skills apparently are not habitual. As already suggested, many sports skills are in fact ballistic in nature and from that point of view as near habitual as one can get in the sense that they are probably preprogrammed as a whole. One has to be careful even then with the word 'habit' for even in skills performed in a relatively unchanging environment Bernstein (1967) long ago pointed out:

> Practice does not consist of repeating a single solution to a motor
> problem, but rather consists of repeating the process of solving the
> problem by techniques which are changed and perfected from
> repetition to repetition; practise thus becomes a process of repetition
> without repetition.

Fitts (1964) computer analogy of skill is based on an hierarchical
structuring of movements. The execution of sub-routines—short, fixed,
repeatable series of operations—is controlled by an executive programme
which provides an overall decision framework for flexible, adaptive functions.
Invariant movement sequences exist therefore as sub-routines and may be
incorporated as response components when necessary. The timing and order
of sub-routines vary with the particular activity giving it its unique
characteristics. With the confusion apparent in the proposed *open-closed* skill
continuum as to the relative importance of habit formation, it may be of
more value to consider skills whether 'open' or 'closed' in terms of their
hierarchical organisation, with the environmental regulation affecting the
executive formation and not the individual sub-routines.

In Poulton's definition of 'open' and 'closed' skills he is only talking about
the steering function of environmental information and not about the nature
of the movements the person will make in relation to such information. While
a priori it might be expected that in a relatively predictable environment one
would 'home in' on a reasonably constant or habitual movement pattern,
there is nothing in the previous definition of 'open' and 'closed' skills which
would lead us to expect that this was axiomatic. So that, to talk about 'open'
skills as Knapp (1964) does as being mainly perceptual is to pre-judge the
issue and we must look for evidence which would support or refute such a
proposal.

It would appear that to consider habitual responses as only being present
in so-called 'closed' skills would be erroneous as the work of Higgins and
Spaeth (1972) and Tyldesley (1975) suggests. They are perhaps more overt in
such skills—since there are for any situation less of them. But, if one accepts
the executive programme idea of Fitts (1964), or Konorski's (1967) Gnostic
units, then habitual responses are present but less easily observable—since for
any 'open' skill situation there are more of them. Their very presence in many
ball game situations for example, enables us to talk about performance *styles*.
It is therefore suggested that my (Whiting, 1972) earlier proposal that:

> . . . many skills classified on Knapp's continuum as being 'open' may in
> fact include movements which are themselves 'closed' in the sense that
> they are un-influenced by the monitoring of environmental information.

is more meaningful. Here is where confusion begins in terminology, for such 'closed' skills are really examples of open-loop behaviour. They are thus 'open' in the sense that it is necessary to monitor information from the environment to determine which movements to select and when and where to trigger them off, but the movement is then not under the steering function of feedback information. The question then becomes whether in 'closed' skills there is a single ballistic or habitual response and whether in open skills there are many response patterns and to what extent these are habitual. It will be appreciated that there is a major problem for training here, for if in so-called open fast ball skills we are to have a variety of executive movement patterns related to changing environmental demands and yet each of these is to be consistent to a particular repeated demand from the environment, it is unlikely that there will be a tremendous number of different ballistic movements which are also consistent.

Learning and Performance

What then are the problems when outcome measures are used as the indices of skill level or of learning? Very often, there is no problem. At other

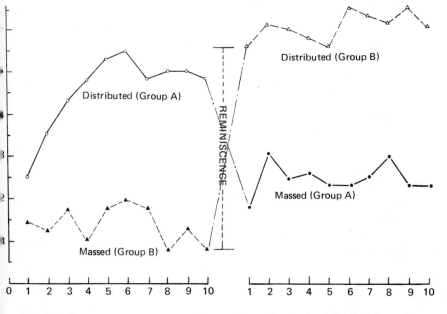

Fig. 6. Performance outcome curves under conditions of massed and distributed practice.

times, the outcome of a person's movements is a very poor indicator of skill level. The reader will recall many instances in which what is known about a person's skill level from protracted experience is not reflected for example by his results under competitive conditions. Situational and personal variables in some way prevent the manifestation of the skilfulness of the person. Classically the difference is demonstrated in massed and distributed practice laboratory situations.

Fig. 6 shows performance outcome curves under conditions of massed and distributed practice on a Minnesota Rate of Manipulation task. Although massed practice depresses the outcome of performance, the fact that learning is not adversely affected is apparent when the massed group after a rest period are transferred on to distributed practice. Furthermore, it is worth emphasising that it *is* movement outcome which is being measured—in this case how many pegs are turned over.

You will note also that what have been shown are outcome curves and not learning curves as are sometimes still mistakenly shown. Performance is overt—learning covert.

How could we show changes in performance? By superimposed force-time traces? Cinephotography? By taking particular performance parameters and illustrating their progressive development? What do we mean by learning having taken place in relation to the performance outcome? What has been learned?

The points being made here are critical ones with far wider implications than those already made. As Wilberg (1972) so forcibly states:

> The second problem, the more fundamental of the two, is related to the fact that the generally used positive performance and error measures only describe the results of performance. Such measures *describe* but never *explain* performance.

They are what are called by Wilberg, *static* measures. It is not the reliability or validity of such measures which is being called into question, but their usefulness in explaining performance. Thus, number of goals scored, number of hits made, time taken to complete a given distance etc. can be stated independently of the performance of the people concerned, i.e. such criteria are not necessarily related to good performance.

There is a solution of course in terms of dynamic rather than static measures which are *performance* rather than *result* oriented. In particular, cinematographical analysis of one kind or another has often been used. Wilberg (1972) comments:

> The change from static to dynamic measures was undoubtedly motivated by a lack of relationship between static measures and the full

length performance. By using dynamic measures, both the direction and degree of modification necessary can be established.

The trouble with dynamic measures of this kind usually relates to the instrumentation involved, the interference of such instrumentation with the subject's performance and the protracted period of time necessary for analysis. At a more simple level, the systems analytic model of human performance (page 10) introduced by Welford (1968), Crossman (1965) Fitts and Posner (1967) and elaborated by Whiting (1969) in relation to ball skill acquisition is fundamentally designed to focus attention on explanatory concepts. What we are presented with in the teaching situation, is descriptive data whereas our interest centres primarily around explanations of such data. What we see is inappropriate movement. All too often, we are inclined to assume that the person who produces a poor performance is incapable, in the sense of not having the potential to produce highly skilled movements. As Connolly (1969) reminds us:

> Failure or great difficulty on the part of a child to learn a given response has frequently been accounted for in terms of the child's not being ready or not being able to learn the response at the time whereas more concern should be centred around the efficiency of the teaching techniques adopted.

It is important therefore to have an understanding of the many systems which contribute towards successful performance and to appreciate that a breakdown may occur in any of these systems. The model presented in Section 1 (Fig. 4) can be used to roughly illustrate the point.

Assuming for example that the skill to be performed requires the taking in of information from the display for its correct performance, a number of disturbances may affect the ability of the performer to do so adequately. In the first place, the performer may fail to orientate himself towards that part of the display where necessary information can be found. This may be due to lack of experience in similar situations, i.e. to a failure in the conceptual framework of the memory store or a failure on the part of the filter systems to extract the relevant information from the totality impinging on the perceptual systems. In part, this could imply a defect in the receptors themselves and certainly such systems should form part of any initial check.

It is possible for the learner to focus his attention on the right part of the display from which the relevant information is available, but to put a wrong interpretation on the sensory input selected—a failure in the perceptual mechanisms influenced by memory stores. This is most clearly shown in the presence of well-known illusions, but it would seem likely that it is more generally applicable. Another interpretation in this case might be the inaccessibility of the memory trace. That is to say, that the learner has experienced the situation previously and has stored data to that effect but is unable to call it up at the right time—either because it is literally inaccessible or because the time taken to recall makes it no longer applicable to the particular situation.

To push the example on further. The subject may orientate himself in the right direction, select and put the correct interpretation on the incoming sensory input but make a wrong translation. That is to say that he makes an inappropriate response. Reasons for this may again rest with limited experience resulting in a failure to build-up stimulus-response compatabilities. Again, the procedure may be carried out effectively even up to the correct translation but the muscular system may be incapable of carrying out the directions of the effector mechanisms so that intention is not matched by outcome.

It is unlikely that the hypothetical situations described do in fact exist in such a clear-cut way. What seems more probable, is that a failure in any one part of the system will affect the development of other parts. That is to say, that a reciprocal relationship probably exists between the various sub-systems such that gross disturbances at least will lead to a lowered capacity for acquiring skill of any kind.

Subjectivity—objectivity

One of the general problems implicit in the discussion so far, relates to the subjectivity—objectivity continuum, in relation to which the study of human movement provides interesting examples which are relevant to the difficulties of evaluation in the skill domain. Judging gymnastics, swimming or similar competitions, are examples with which the reader will be familiar and therefore on which there is little point in my digressing at this stage.

The problem is very apparent in physical education where terms like:

    objective/subjective
    qualitative/quantitative
    art of movement/science of movement

tend to be polarised and used as if they were discrete categories.

Is evaluation in the art of movement for example non-objective, or is it less objective than in the scientific study of movement? Could we not look at the art of movement in a scientific way? Are techniques for the analysis of human movement essentially objective, scientific procedures or can we talk about some techniques which are essentially more subjective in nature; And moreover, is such subjectivity inherent in the system or is it simply a reflection of the limitations in our own knowledge and instrumentation. Presumably in any aspect of research we are being subjective because we cannot be more objective? Or are we? This depends upon our stance and certainly in everyday life situations perhaps we could not care less about being objective. Perhaps subjectivity is a peculiarly desirable quality in certain events—selecting a wife or husband for example! Or perhaps nearer home, some would maintain this to be the case in the field of aesthetic experience.

Unfortunately, scientific method is often looked upon as a sacred cow with absolute objectivity being its sole criterion. But, the fact that observation is of primary importance in all scientific endeavour should caution against the acceptance of objectivity as some absolute. As Meredith (1966) put it:

> Since every observation occurs at a definite moment of time, under particular historic conditions, the physical pattern of stimulation can never recur precisely. We thus have two difficulties in accepting the assurance that scientific laws are both 'objective' and 'constant' for all the data on which they are based is subjective and variable.

This was brought home particularly in a recent short article by Poulton (1973) on bias in ergonomic experiments:

> In a within-subject experimental design, each person receives a number of conditions in a balanced or random order. The design produces assymetrical transfer and range effects. Yet practically all ergonomic recommendations are based upon the results of experiments which use this kind of design. The recommendations need to be checked, using separate groups of people for each experimental condition.

Similar problems have been highlighted under the general rubric 'Rosenthal Effect' and 'Hawthorne Effect'. Currently researchers are turning their attention towards the 'Hidden Curriculum' implicit in the concept of styles previously outlined and the concept of 'packaging' recently developed by Wilberg (1973).

Personality Assessment

Not only do we have skilled performers but we also have skilled observers of movement. One interesting field which is receiving considerable attention currently is that of personality assessment through movement, although it must have been a procedure adopted since time immemorial. The major exponents in this country of recent years, have been Lamb (1965) and North

(1973). On the face of it, movement characteristics if they can be suitably isolated and categorised would seem to be useful indicators of stable personality traits and their accurate assessment a highly skilful procedure. The problem is, that no two people really seem to be able to agree on the assessment of such factors of movement behaviour in the systems currently being advocated. This may be due the reader might argue to the lack of experience and training of suitable movement assessors. Now, it is true that people trained to look out for particular characteristics can become skilled in doing so and in consequence do have closer agreement in their assessment, but is this the result of seeing what they expect or want to see rather than of objectively analysing the information in front of them? Let us take examples of what I mean:

1 The major critique of Sheldon and Stevens (1942) work on personality centres around the subjective nature of the assessment i.e. the limitations of the assessment procedures and also the subjectivity involved. For example, in linking his personality assessments to morphological characteristics, Sheldon spent a period of about nine months evaluating the life-history of his subject and then correlating the observed personality manifestations with the assessed body-type. Now, the point here, is the stereotypic knowledge that the person assessing the body-type had about associated personality characteristics and one would want to know how the one influenced the other. This particular problem has been highlighted by recent studies such as those of Dibiase and Hjelle (1968). They were concerned with the problem of the *kind* of body considered desirable to possess. For example, in reviewing the literature in this area, they suggest that characteristic body-builds elicit steurotyped reactions from both children and adults when they are asked to rate particular somatotypes in terms of personality traits. The meso-morph image is usually perceived as socially and personally favourable and the ectomorph image as having traits which are socially submissive and personally unfavourable i.e. assessors are already predisposed, 'set', expectant of certain characteristics.

2 Let us take another example, this time from the vexed field of art. This time, I rely heavily on an article by Koestler (1964) on snobbery in art:

In 1948, a German art restorer named Dietrich Fey, engaged in reconstruction work on Lubeck's ancient St. Marien Church, stated that his workmen had discovered traces of Gothic wall-paintings dating back to the thirteenth century under a coating of chalk on the church walls. The restoration of the paintings was entrusted to

Fey's assistant, Lothar Malskat, who finished the job two years later. In 1950 Chancellor Adenauer presided over the ceremonies marking the completion of the restoration work in the presence of art experts from all parts of Europe. Their unanimous opinion, voiced by Chancellor Adenauer, was that the twenty-one thirteenth-century Gothic saints on the church walls were 'a valuable treasure and a fabulous discovery of lost masterpieces!

None of the experts on that or any later occasion expressed doubt as to the authenticity of the frescoes. It was Herr Malskat himself who, two years later, disclosed the fraud. He presented himself on his own initiative at Lubeck police headquarters, where he stated that the frescoes were entirely his own work undertaken by order of his boss, Herr Fey; and he asked to be tried for forgery. The leading German art experts, however stuck to their opinion; the frescoes, they said, were without doubt genuine, and Herr Malskat was merely seeking cheap publicity. An official board of enquiry was appointed and came to the conclusion that the restoration of the wall paintings was a hoax—but only after Herr Malskat had confessed that he had also manufactured hundreds of Rembrandts, Watteaus, Toulouse-Lautrecs, Picassos, Henri Rousseaus, Cortos, Chagalls, Vlamincks and other masters and sold them as originals—some of which were actually found by the police in Herr Fey's house. Without this corpus delecti, it is doubtful whether the German experts would ever have admitted having been fooled.

The point being made here, is that man generally looks at nature through coloured glasses even though he may not be conscious of so doing. In a similar way, our whole manner of perceiving human movement depends upon our ideas about its purpose or function. In Koestler's terms, on the selective code which determines our criteria of significance and patterns our vision.

References

BERNSTEIN, N. (1967). *The Coordination and Regulation of Movements.* London: Pergamon.

BEST, D. (1975). The aesthetic in sport. *J. Hum. Mov. Studies,* 1,

BROADBENT, D.E. (1971). Cognitive psychology: introduction. *British Medical Bulletin,* 27, 191-194.

CONNOLLY, K. (1969). The application of operant conditioning to the measurement and development of motor skill in children. *Developmental medicine and Child Neurology*, **10**, 697-705.

CROSSMAN, E.R.F.W. (1964). Information processing in human skill. *British Medical Bulletin*, **20**, 32-37.

DIBIASE, W.J. & HJELLE, L.A. (1968). Body-image stereotypes and body-type preferences among male college students. *Perceptual and Motor Skills*, **27**, 1143-1146.

FITTS, P.M. (1964). Skill learning. In A.W. Melton (Ed.) *Categories of Human Learning*. New York: Academic Press.

FITTS, P.M. & POSNER, M.I. (1967). *Human Performance*. Belmont: Brooks/Cole.

GLENCROSS, D.J. (1973). Temporal organisation in a repetitive speed skill. *Ergonomics*, **16**, 765-776.

GREGORY, R.L. (1970). On how so little information controls so much behaviour. *Ergonomics*, **13**, 236-247.

GUTHRIE, E.R. (1952). *The Psychology of Learning*. New York: Harper & Row.

HAMMOND, W. (1975). A systems-analysis of fencing. In H.T.A. Whiting (Ed.) *Readings in Human Performance*. London: Lepus Books.

HIGGINS, J.R. & SPAETH, Ree, K. (1972). Relationship between consistency of movement and environmental condition. *Quest*, **17**, 61-69.

JONES, M.G. (1972). Perceptual characteristics and athletic performance. In H.T.A. Whiting (Ed.) *Readings in Sports Psychology*. London: Kimpton.

KNAPP, B.N. (1961). A note on skill. *Occup. Psychol.*, **35**, 76-78.

KNAPP, B.N. (1964). *Skill in Sport*. London: Routledge & Kegan Paul.

KOESTLER, A. (1964). *The Act of Creation*. London: Hutchinson.

KONORSKI, J. (1967). *The Integrative Activity of the Brain*. Chicago: University Press.

LAMB, W. (1965). *Posture and Gesture*. London: Duckworth.

MANAHAN, J.E. (1972). Formulation of the motor plan. *Quest*, **17**, 46-51.

MEREDITH, G.P. (1966). *Instruments of Communication*. Oxford: Pergamon.

NEVEROVICH, Y.Z. (1958). Experimental work quoted by A.V. Zaporozhets. In N. O'Connor (Ed.) *Recent Soviet Psychology*. London: Pergamon.

NORTH, M. (1973). *Personality Assessment through Movement*. London: Macdonald & Evans.

POULTON, E.C. (1950). Anticipation in open and closed sensorimotor skills. Unpublished paper, A.P.U. Cambridge.

POULTON, E.C. (1951). On prediction in skilled movements. *Psychological Bulletin*, **54**, 467-478.

POULTON, E.C. (1973). Bias in ergonomic experiments. *Applied Ergonomics,* **4**, 17-18.

RICOEUR, P. (1966). *Freedom and Nature: the voluntary and involuntary.* North Western University Press.

RYLE, G. (1969). *The Concept of the Mind.* London: Hutchinson.

SEASHORE, R.H. (1951). In S.S. Stevens (Ed.) *Handbook of Experimental Psychology.* New York: Wiley.

SHELDON, W.H. & STEVENS, S.S. (1942). *The Varieties of Temperament.* New York: Harper.

TYLDESLEY, D. (1975). The programming of movements. Unpublished Ph.D. thesis, Department of Physical Education, University of Leeds.

WELFORD, A.T. (1968). *Fundamentals of Skill.* London: Methuen.

WHITING, H.T.A. (1969). *Acquiring Ball Skill: a psychological interpretation.* London: Bell.

WHITING, H.T.A. (1972). Theoretical models for an understanding of perceptual-motor skill. *Quest,* **17**, 24-34.

WILBERG, R.B. (1972). Assignment and measurement of performance. Unpublished paper presented conference of the British Society of Sports Psychology, Leeds.

WILBERG, R.B. (1973). 'Packaging'. Proceedings of the 1st. Canadian Congress on Sports Sciences, Montreal.

WRIGHT, D.S. (1967). *Introducing Psychology.* Harmondsworth: Penguin.

3

ABILITY
AND SKILL

3 ABILITY AND SKILL

There are problems—particularly semantic ones—in linking together the concepts of *ability* and *skill*. Although at least one worker in the field has made a clear distinction between abilities and skill, there are terminological difficulties which need to be discussed before looking at possible interpretations. Perhaps the most confusing issue if we want to dichotomise *skill* and *ability(ies)* is the fact that they are often used synonymously. Thus, in one of the most oft-quoted definitions of *skill,* Knapp (1964) extrapolating from the work of Guthrie (1952) talks about:

> ... the learned *ability* to bring about predetermined results with maximum certainty often with the minimum outlay of time or energy or both.

Skill of *ability* in this sense, is judged by success in bringing about the predetermined result or goal and as such is a relative term. (This in itself gives rise to problems of evaluation which were raised in Section 2). The reader is also reminded of the assertion in Section 1 that we do not observe *skill* directly but infer its presence by the behaviour of the person and that a concept of this nature is known in the psychological literature as an *intervening variable.* That is to say, it is not directly observed, but is defined operationally by a set of independent and dependent variables which *are* observable. Movement or its outcome is what is actually observed and measured.

Thus, we may have *skill* in relation to a number of different *skills* where the latter are defined in terms of predetermined goals. The acquisition of such skill is the result of a protracted period of learning.

It might at this stage therefore be asked what has to be learned in a new situation or what are the prerequisites for acquiring a new skill? Ultimately of course, the objective is to modify the movement patterns of the body to bring about the predetermined end result. Can it be said therefore that what are learned are the movements necessary to achieve the end result? The problem here, revolves around the use of the term movements. In Section 1, it was suggested that skilled behaviour involved the effective ordering and hierarchical structuring of sub-routines. The assumption being made here was that sub-routines—the elemental routinised movements—necessary for construction of any complex movement patterns which we would normally look upon as examples of skilled behaviour were already present in the system. So that, when we talk about people learning the movements necessary to achieve the end result, we are implying that by gradual refinement, the person learns to link together the appropriate *sub-routines* in the right sequential order and correct temporal relationships. While the question of how the sub-routines are learned is an important one, it is not to be developed here but the reader is reminded that this topic would be of central importance under the rubric 'significance of movement for development' discussed in Section 4. Generally speaking in a skill learning situation, the assumption is made that the sub-routines necessary for the new movements are present in the system. (There would seem to be little point in requiring anyone to learn a particular skill when the necessary sub-routines had never been acquired). What has to be learned, and what will be altered as skill develops, is the *relative attractiveness* of particular movement patterns which will be determined amongst other things by the adequacy of knowledge of results (feedback) which follows on any attempt at the new movement pattern, the amount of practice which has taken place and the person's capacity for improvement.

What we are saying then is that one of the prerequisites for acquiring a new skill involving overt actions is the presence of the necessary sub-routines in the system. This however is to place the problem in its simplest form, for in many skill situations there is a need to monitor information from the environment often involving a rapidly changing display in order to select the appropriate sub-routines and to learn to organise and coordinate them in such a way that they meet the changing demands of the environment. It is this capacity to process information of diverse kinds (as well as the possession of diverse sub-routines) in order to make one's behaviour adaptive—that is goal-directed rather than random—that gives rise to the need to postulate 'abilities' as distinct from skill.

Take for example a child being required to catch a ball. The movements involved are relatively simple and consist of moving the hand to an interception position and closing the hands around the ball. Even the child of a very young age has little difficulty in reaching up and grasping the ball of appropriate size suspended from a string (particularly if no time constraints are imposed and the assessment of success is based purely on being able to graps the ball at some stage). Similar movements are required in the actual catching situation but there are vastly more constraints in such a dynamic changing environment. Basically the fundamentals of the skill are twofold:

1   To move the hand into an interception position.
2   To close the fingers at the appropriate time.

In order to move the hand into an interception position, the child will need to know:

1   where it is initially i.e. to have competence in spatial visualisation—a position sense
2   where it will be i.e. to know something about parabolic flight paths of a ball and how they are affected by wind, ball-spin etc.

In order to close his fingers at the right time, the child will need to know:

1   the time at which the ball will reach his hand i.e. to know about velocity and possibly acceleration prediction in order to know how to time the onset of his response.
2   the limitations of his reaction time particularly if the catching task is severly time-constrained.

Or to take a less subjective example provided by the National Aeronautics and Space Administration study carried out by Parker et al (1965). This was concerned with the development of an integrated battery of tests to measure the primary dimensions of perceptual-motor performance appropriate for the Gemini mission. Eighteen basic perceptual-motor abilities were identified and classified into four categories.

1   Fine Manipulative Abilities
    Arm-Hand Steadiness
        Hold arm and hand steady while fully extended
    Wrist-Finger Speed
        Make rapid, repetitive tapping movements
    Finger Dexterity
        Manipulate small objects with fingers
    Manual Dexterity
        Manipulate large objects with hand
2   Gross Positioning and Movement Abilities
    Position Estimation
        Reach for specific locations without use of vision
    Response Orientation
        Make appropriate directional response to non-spatial stimulus
    Control Precision
        Make fine, controlled positioning movements
    Speed of Arm Movement

Make discrete, rapid arm movements
Multilimb Coordination
Use hands and/or feet simultaneously
Position Reproduction
Repeat discrete arm-hand movement without aid of vision
3   System Equalisation Abilities
Movement Analysis
Differentiate target velocity and acceleration
Movement Prediction
Integrate target motion components to estimate future target position
Rate Control
Control vehicle having first-order system dynamics
Acceleration Control
Control vehicle having second-order system dynamics
4   Perceptual-Cognitive Abilities
Perceptual Speed
Make rapid visual comparisons of display elements
Time Sharing
Divide attention among several displays
Reaction-Time
Respond as rapidly as possible to discrete signal
Mirror Tracing
Use mirror-image display to perform directional hand-arm movements

In both examples, the concept of abilities has been superficially outlined. It is suggested that their development in the subject are *prerequisites* for successful performance of many different skills. They are not generally task specific. Fleishman (1964) in particular makes this distinction between 'skill' and 'abilities' as follows:

The term 'skill' refers to the level of proficiency on a specific task or a limited group of tasks. As we use the term skill, it is task-oriented. When we talk about proficiency in flying an aeroplane, in operating a turret lathe, or in playing basketball, we are talking about a specific skill. . .

The assumption is that skills involved in complex activities can be described in terms of more basic abilities. For example, the level of performance a man can attain on a turret lathe may depend on his basic abilities of manual dexterity and motor coordination. However these same abilities may be important to proficiency in other skills as well.

Thus manual dexterity is needed in assembling electrical components and motor coordination is needed to fly an aeroplane.

What are these abilities to which Fleishman refers?:

> Ability refers to a more general trait of the individual which has been inferred from certain response consistencies (e.g. correlations) on certain kinds of tasks. These are fairly enduring traits which in the adult are more difficult to change. Many of these abilities are, of course, themselves the product of learning, and develop at different rates *mainly during childhood and adolescence*. Some abilities (e.g. colour vision) depend more on genetic than learning factors, but most abilities depend on both to some degree. In any case, at a given stage in life, they represent traits which the individual brings with him when he begins to learn a new task.
>
> These abilities are related to performance in a variety of human tasks. For example, the fact that spatial visualisation has been found related to performance on such diverse tasks as aerial navigation and dentistry, makes this ability somehow more basic.

A regression has therefore been made from the descriptive definition of skill to some of the factors which influence its development. Later it will be necessary to regress a further stage and ask what factors affect the development of abilities!

Abilities then are individual difference variables and have been found useful as classification procedures in relation to for example compensatory education procedures. The other two psychological trait modalities are *temperament* and *motivation*. While there is an interaction between the three modalities in the sense that personality and motivation enter into the development of abilities and consequently abilities shape personality and motivation, there are marked differences both in their evaluation and modus operandi and they should not be confused (Cattell, 1971).

One of Fleishman's key points in his definition of an ability was:

> . . . a more general trait of the individual which has been inferred from certain response consistencies on certain kinds of task.

It is this concept of *generality* which again had led to a lot of confusion in the literature. Just how general is general? This has been a particular controversy in relation to the concept of *general motor ability* which in the past people have purported to be able to measure. To some extent this was a reflection of the different models of cognitive development put forward by the American and British schools. While the British contingent tended to stress a hierarchical structure of abilities with major emphasis on a 'g' factor, the American school gave primary attention to a multifactorial approach such factors being relatively general i.e. contributing to a number of different aspects of human performance but not embracing the totality. More recently, Cattell (1971) has pointed out that a general factor is, in any case only a mathematician's term, applicable to a particular matrix operation and not to scientific concepts. What we really have in psychology are factors of varying breadth. A so-called 'g' factor is retained for the broadest factor. It is a question of usefulness which probably decides the issue. The percentage of variance accounted for favouring an emphasis on a multifactorial rather than a 'g' approach.

On the question of the specificity or generality of the abilities required to perform psychomotor tasks, Yates (1968) suggests that the long line of experimental results stretching from Seashore et al (1940) to Fleishman (1954) produce agreement on the fact that:

> Although a general factor of psychomotor ability cannot be doubted its importance has generally been rejected.

The solution preferred has been that which rests upon relatively independent group factors, clusters of these group factors entering into the performance of different skills. Mention should perhaps be made of the fact that the majority of factorial studies in this area have been carried out with highly selected groups for special purposes. Many of Fleishman's most sophisticated studies for example have been carried out in an attempt to devise prognostic tests for highly skilled positions in the American forces. This is not to deny the usefulness of the studies, but to merit caution in extrapolating to other populations. Again, the abilities isolated by different workers are not necessarily definitive. They are dependent as are all these kinds of study upon the nature of the test batteries used. These have differed widely from study to study.

So far, a distinction has been made between skill and abilities and the concept of general ability and its usefulness has been discussed. It has been proposed that skilled performance depends upon abilities which are present before embarking on the task together with habits and subskills which are peculiar to and acquired within the task itself. Fleishman (1967) makes the point that some narrow *abilities* are also task specific and may only be acquired by performance of *that* task.

If the ideas discussed so far are accepted, it follows that the individual who has a great many highly developed basic abilities *can* become proficient at a great variety of specific tasks. Transfer of training is implicit in the extent to which such tasks share common abilities.

In some skills, abilities which contribute to performance early in the learning process are not necessarily the same abilities which contribute to later performance. This is reflected in the following statement and should be a sobering thought to those 'experts' in particular skill areas who attempt to teach the beginner on the basis of what the expert performer is known or assumed to do. Fleishman (1967) comments:

> The ability-skill paradigm and the experimental results based on it is consistent with an information processing model of human learning. Abilities can be thought of as 'capacities for utilising different kinds of information'. Thus, individuals who are especially good at using certain types of spatial information, make rapid progress in the early stages of learning certain kinds of motor tasks, while individuals sensitive to proprioceptive cues do better in tasks requiring precise motor control.

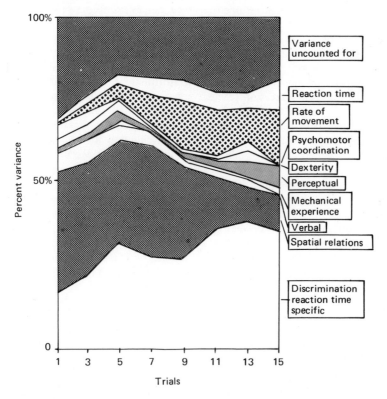

Fig. 7. Percentage of variance represented by each factor at different stages of practice on the discrimination reaction time task. (Fleishman & Hempel, 1955).

The position is illustrated in Fig. 7 for a two-hand coordination task. It is not entirely clear what relationship these abilities have to what Fleishman variously terms, 'spatial orientation' or 'spatial visualisation', these being referred to as 'general abilities'. Although Fleishman does not raise the point in his review, it is worth asking whether or not the ability to utilise spatial or proprioceptive information is in some ways different or more basic than other abilities listed? He does, however, point out that some abilities may be required in most skills. These are abilities that are related to the organisation of responses.

Of primary concern in the present context is the contribution of particular activities to the development of abilities rather than the teaching of specific skills dependent upon such abilities. Implicit within this idea, is the concept of the *age of readiness*.

If we accept that the possession of abilities is vital to the efficient learning of a skill, then we either assume that it is a valuable procedure to deliberately attempt to cultivate the development of such abilities *prior* to the skill being attempted or we assume that by teaching children specific skills we are at the same time developing abilities which can be used both in the attainment of that skill and which will carry over into other skills where the same kinds of information processing take place. Unfortunately, the majority of our specialist physical education teachers are trained for secondary school work. One sometimes gets the impression that structured physical education begins at eleven years of age. Yet at the same time we hear the repeated complaint that children coming up from the primary school to the secondary school have such widely divergent 'abilities' (in the old sense!). We have also made the point that many of the abilities which contribute towards successful skill performance are developed in early childhood. We might ask therefore what can education in general and physical education in particular contribute towards the development of abilities and what emphasis should be placed on such development and at what ages, rather than on the learning of specific skills? This would not mean that we do not teach specific skills but rather that we would be less concerned with the outcome and more with the contribution such experience was making to the development of the child in terms of the development of abilities.

Surprisingly, we have to look to compensatory education procedures for this kind of approach. For example, from the original work of Oseretsky (1929) through the various revisions (Yarmolenko, 1933; Doll, 1946; Sloan, 1948; 1955) down to the work of Stott (1966) there has been an attempt to isolate the factors underlying the particular deficiencies of impaired children. Some workers even attempt to map out a hierarchy of abilities. Sapir and Wilson (1967) for example suggest that specific compensatory education should be tailored to the needs of each child and further point out that the individual patterns of deficit differ so widely that differential diagnosis is an essential pre-requisite for appropriate remedial work. A diagnostic profile is built up of the child's deficiencies and then a programme arranged to assist in each of the areas. Their results indicate that certain areas of deficit are more common than others e.g. directionality/laterality, spatial relations, visuo-motor, auditory design. If this turns out to be a more general finding, attention should be concentrated on these areas. It would also appear to be necessary, following on from Fleishman's work, to discover the extent to which proficiency in these areas is involved in the performance of the widest range of everyday skills required by children from a number of socio-economic groupings. These abilities might then be developed in pre-school, 'headstart' and early junior classes. For, the implication here, is that an 'age of readiness' for learning particular skills is a meaningful concept, such an age being dependent on the level of particular abilities in the child relevant to the task in question.

To take an example from another culture, Biesheuvel (1963) has discussed the limitations imposed by lack of opportunity for learning particular skills in relation to African populations. He suggests that failure to provide the right psychomotor experience at particular stages will prevent the full realisation of potential ability. He raises the interesting proposition as to whether limited

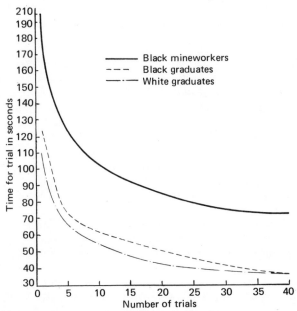

Fig. 8. Performance of criterian grouped on a two-handed coordination task. (Biesheuvel, 1963)

opportunities for learning certain basic movement habits in the tribal or urban African environment may be responsible for the difficulties which native Africans experience in acquiring the manual dexterity needed for certain skilled trades. The discrepancy which exists between the performance of tribesmen and educated white or African groups is illustrated in Fig. 8. Biesheuvel suggests that a prima facie case exists for providing African children with more opportunity to manipulate, to diversify their motor responses and habits and to exercise their basic skills more continually.

The key question raised by these examples, is 'should a concentration on abilities' be confined to compensatory education programmes—even supposing that these exist in school or should a more positive approach be taken in deliberately structuring experience to provide for the development of a wide range of such abilities particularly during the early developmental years?

Some thoughts on the ways in which the development of abilities might be brought about are discussed in a more general context in the next section.

References

BIESHEUVEL, S. (1963). The growth of abilities and character. *S.Afr.J.Sc.*, **59**, 375-385.

CATTELL, R.B. (1971). *Abilities, Their Structure, Growth, and Action.* Boston: Houghton Mifflin.

DOLL, E.A. (1946). The Oseretsky scale. *Am. J. Ment. Def.*, **50**, 485-487.

FLEISHMAN, E.A. (1954). Dimensional analysis of psychomotor abilities. *J. Exp. Psychol.*, XLVIII, 437-454.

FLEISHMAN, E.A. (1964). *The Structure and Measurement of Physical Fitness.* New Jersey: Prentice-Hall.

FLEISHMAN, E.A. (1967). Individual differences and motor learning. In Gagne, R.M. (Ed.) *Learning and Individual Differences.* Ohio: Merrill.

GUTHRIE, E.R. (1952). *The Psychology of Learning.* New York: Harper & Row.

KNAPP, B. (1964). *Skill in Sport.* London: Routledge & Kegan Paul.

OSERETSKY, N.A. (1929). A group method of examining the motor functioning of children and adolescents. *Z. Kinderfersch*, **35**, 332-372.

PARKER, J.F., Jr., REILLY, D.E., DILLON, R.F., ANDREWS, T.G. & FLEISHMAN, E.A. (1965). Development of tests for measurement of primary perceptual-motor performance. NASA CR – 335.

SAPIR, G.S. & WILSON, B.M. (1967). Patterns of developmental deficits. *Percept. & Motor Skills,* **24**, 1291-1293.

SEASHORE, R.H., BUXTON, C.E. & MCCOLLAN, I.M. (1940). Multiple factorial analysis of fine motor skills. *Am. J. Psychol.,* **53**, 251-259.

SLOAN, W. (1948). *Lincoln Adaptation of the Oseretsky Scale.* Illinois: Lincoln.

SLOAN, W. (1955). The Lincoln-Oseretsky motor developmental scale. *Genetic Psychol. Monog.,* **51**, 182-252.

STOTT, D.H. (1966). A general test of motor impairment for children. *Dev. Med. Child. Neur.,* **8**, 523-531.

YARMOLENKO, A. (1933). The motor sphere of school children. *J. Genet. Psychol.,* **42**, 298-316.

YATES, P.T. (1968). Abnormalities of psychomotor functions. In H.J. Eysenck (Ed.) *Handbook of Abnormal Psychology.* London: Pergamon.

4

THE SIGNIFICANCE OF MOVEMENT FOR EARLY DEVELOPMENT

4 THE SIGNIFICANCE OF MOVEMENT FOR EARLY DEVELOPMENT

Movement and Activities

This Section is concerned with the significance of *movement* and not *activities* for development. It is important therefore at the outset to establish the difference between these two concepts and at the same time to emphasise that the possible significance of participation in *activities* for development is not being denigrated.

The distinction being made is helped by a consideration of the concepts *movement* and *behaviour*. As Alston (1974) states:

> . . . whatever else it may include, the category of behaviour has from the beginning been designed to range over familiar examples of human action. The 'science of behaviour' is explicitly intended to provide a theoretical understanding (explanation) of the things we *do* in daily life. . . In view of these repeated protestations it comes as a shock to realise that comparatively little psychological research is concerned with hypotheses and theories, the dependent variables of which have to do with human action.

Thus, Alston is not equating human action necessarily with human movement. The dichotomy he makes between intentional and unintentional actions is illustrated in Fig. 9.

It is overt actions defined by Alston as:

> . . . actions that involve publicly observable bodily movements.

with which we are concerned here, not because they are of direct importance, but because they are the context for the dependent or independent variable with which we are concerned i.e. human movement. The distinction is perhaps clarified by Hutt (1974) who writes:

73

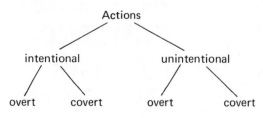

Fig. 9. Action Concepts.

Behaviour is not movement and to specify an action in terms of muscle activity or extension/flexion of limbs is not a specification in terms of behaviour. Categories of behaviour are defined both morphologically and functionally i.e. in terms of their appearance as well as by their effects or context. In other words it is meaningful to use 'painting' as a behaviour category despite the fact that the motor patterns may vary over time and over individuals, whereas it is distinctly unhelpful to describe the activity in terms of discrete movements such as flexion of the digits or lateral displacement of the forearm. Identification of the motor constituents of a behaviour category is by no means the same as using those movements to reconstruct the behaviour.

Human movement then derives its meaning from its context but it is with the *movement* in context that we are concerned and not with the context itself. This idea can perhaps be clarified still further by reference to a book shortly to be published in the Human Movement Series (paradoxically) entitled 'Work and Leisure'. While clearly human movement is crucial to both these broad contexts the book as such has almost nothing to say about movement! In a similar way, there has often been a professional confusion between human *movement* and *activities*. While we may study (or appreciate) human movement in the context of an activity (e.g. the movements made in playing Golf or by children playing Hop-scotch) it is clearly also possible to study or look for the significance of the *activity* itself independent of the movements involved (as happens for example in the so-called Sociology of Sport). We are not here concerned with this level of analysis.

The dichotomy elaborated reflects the progress of a new field of study which is now passing from the embryo stage to that of rapid development. While it would not be possible to pinpoint with any degree of accuracy its emergence as a separate field of study, it is clear that the past five years in particular has seen an acceleration both in interest and published material from diverse sources (Brooke and Whiting, 1972). Such information is of interest to aestheticians, biomechanics, choreographers, educationists, engineers, ergonomists, paediatricians, psychologists and other students of human movement.

Having said this, the suggestion is made that the primary interest in this field of study by the educationist concerned with the development of the very young child will be the *significance* of movement for development in general—cognitive, physical, social. With the older child (both in chronological and maturational terms) such a concern may well shift towards the significance of particular *activities* in which the contribution of movement per se is incidental. In this Section therefore I am concerned to raise a number of topics for consideration rather than attempting to structure the field. It is hoped that such ideas may stimulate the reader to expand his knowledge by literature and empirical research orientated under the rubric Significance of Movement for Development.

Early development

While verbal education plays a dominant role in our formal educational system, it must be realised that there is an important developmental period prior to the manifestation of verbal ability when the child's interaction with his environment is mediated by other systems and in particular the motor systems.

The importance of early movement behaviour is reflected in Piaget's (1955) hierarchical stages of cognitive development. It is Piaget's belief—based on extended observation—that for cognitive development to take place, it is necessary for the schemata which would normally be developed at each stage to be acquired before progress can be made to the next stage. It will be realised that the sensory-motor stage for Piaget extends from nought to about eighteen months of age—that is to say, until language begins to be developed. It is characterised by the exploring of concrete objects by movement and establishing the permanence of such objects. Bower (1974) puts a similar emphasis on pre-language experience:

> I think it is generally agreed that infancy, the period before language, is one of the most critical segments of human development. During infancy the basic human motor skills are established, perceptual development is virtually completed, and the roots of the cognitive skills that will grow into a human intellect are laid down.

The lack of awareness of many educationalists and of parents of the significance of movement for development is a great pity because it would appear from the discussion that follows, that such an awareness might lead to procedures which resulted in beneficial gains for the child and the prevention of detrimental effects.

Heredity and Environmental Effects

The title 'Significance of movement for development' may suggest to the reader that a strictly environmental effect is being concentrated on to the exclusion of an hereditary potential. This is not necessarily the case, but in as far as hereditary potential needs an environment in which to manifest itself, the emphasis in this paper must be on environmental structuring. It is of course appreciated that in order for any skill to be acquired, the individual must *inherently* have the potential and the environment must provide the opportunity for that particular skill to be developed.

The wide influence of environmental effects on early development are reflected in Connolly's (1971) statement:

> An individual interacts with itself during development. The environment is highly inhomogeneous at all phases of development from the fertilisation of the egg onwards. Roberts and Matthysse (1970) suggest that local environmental conditions may influence the genetic control of the surface property of cells. Neurones may show local differences in surface properties which result from the differential expression of genetic potentialities at any one time.

Some of the impetus for examining possibilities of increasing *cognitive* development has come from the comparatively recent appreciation that intellectual potential as reflected by current performance (particularly in the very early years) is often not a good reflection of developmental possibilities although the *range* over which change may be effected is in the main limited.

An important consideration in this respect, arises out of the work of Fleishman (1967). He has differentiated between *skills* and *abilities* which enter into skilled performance (elaborated in Section 3). A 'skill' to Fleishman is 'the level of proficiency on a specific task or limited group of tasks, whereas 'abilities' are 'mediating processes' between stimulus and response. They refer to 'more general traits of the individual which have been inferred from certain response consistencies on certain kinds of task'. He also refers to abilities as 'capacities for utilising different kinds of information'. Here is a suggestion as to *qualitative* differences in available (to the individual) information. It would seem reasonable that different people would show differential capacities for utilising different kinds of information and this would be dependent upon both heredity and experience. It follows from Fleishman's contention that the individual who has a great many highly developed basic abilities *can* (in the sense of having the possibility to) become proficient at a great variety of specific tasks. In some quarters and in the light of modern thinking about changing demands in relation to quickly developing technologies this might be considered to be highly desirable. The possession of diverse and highly developed abilities would be assumed to lead to transferability across tasks.

Of particular interest is Fleishman's contention that the rate of learning and the final level achieved by particular individuals on certain skills are both limited by the *basic abilities* of these individuals. The question in need of elaboration in the present context, is the significance of movement for the development of particular abilities and how movement experience might be structured with this aim in view.

Consideration of Fleishman's viewpoint also reflects back on the topics of 'critical periods' and 'age of readiness'. If in fact, abilities which may be primarily innate or primarily acquired need to be present before skilled behaviour of any kind can be carried out, it follows that the concept of 'age of readiness' is a meaningful one. The difficulty here, is that it is not clear to what extent exposure to the situation in which particular skills are to occur will lead to the development of the necessary abilities or whether it is more efficacious to concentrate on the building up of the necessary abilities before tackling a particular skill which demands such abilities.

Movement and Intelligence

Consideration of the development of *abilities* raises the interesting question of the nature and contribution of movement to intellectual development. This idea is reflected in the two abstracts which follow. The first is by the physiologist Sherrington (1951):

> It would seem to be the motor act under the 'urge to live' which has been the cradle of the mind. The motor act, mechanically integrating the individual, would seem to have started the mind on its road to respectability. The great collateral branch of life, the plants, despite all its variety and unequalled profusion of types has never in any event developed an animal-like locomotory act, nor a muscle or a nerve, it has likewise remained without recognisable mind. As motor integration proceeds with it, the servant of an urge seeking satisfaction.

Bernstein (1940) echoes this message in proposing that locomotor acts belong to the category of extremely ancient movements; that they are phylogenetically older than the cortical hemispheres and have undoubtedly affected the development of the central nervous system in the same manner as have the distance receptors.

The second abstract comes from a professor of education—the reader might like to speculate as to when it was written:

... the need of children for bodily activity is being increasingly acknowledged in practice, though slowly and somewhat grudgingly. Despite all the indications of nature, children of five years-old and upwards are still made to sit for long hours in desks, mainly looking and listening. Public opinion is satisfied if a few minutes daily be spent in the playground and if, two or three times a week the children be put through some form of bodily drill. Even these deliverances from the desks are however advocated purely from a physical standpoint. Consequently, as long as bodily growth goes on normally everything is regarded as satisfactory. Modern knowledge enables us to go further and to affirm that the relation between body and mind is so intimate and constant that the intelligence is dwarfed whenever the demand for bodily activity is not met.

Welton (?)

One of the difficulties about the last sentence in Welton's quote, is his failure to suggest critical ages at which dwarfing of the intelligence might occur in the absence of suitable movement experience. In view of the work of many developmental psychologists, it will be appreciated that the greatest influence in this respect is likely to come very early in the life of the child when early programming is taking place. Here, a difference is being made between earlier and later learning in the sense that the quality of the early experience in childhood determines to a large extent the child's potential for skill learning of all kinds at some later stage of development. This idea is reflected by Bower (1974) in his recent book and in the context of cognitive skills.

My concern throughout has been to show the importance of the psychological environment of the developing infant in speeding up or slowing down his attainment of fundamental cognitive skills. I believe that infancy is the critical period in cognitive development—the period when the greatest gains and the greatest losses can occur. Further, the gains and losses that occur here become harder to offset with increasing age.

Although evidence of this kind from the field of human behaviour is less conclusive than that from the animal world, it is a viewpoint put forward many years ago by Hebb (1966). He maintained that sensory stimulation from the early environment is necessary for the maintenance of some neural structures which would otherwise degenerate and also for the occurrence of learning which is essential for normal adult behaviour. Early experience was said to build up the 'mediating processes' which once established make possible the very rapid learning of the mature adult.

Although I will not develop the topic here, it is interesting to note that Levine and Mullins (1966) have suggested that certain early experiences may serve to set or 'time' the neuroendocrine system so that later in the organism's life history the threshold and duration of emotional stress reactions are altered.

Connolly (1971) makes an additional salient point:

> Self-stimulation in embryos via proprioceptive feedback following movement may be important, not in the development of fixed action patterns as such, but in ensuring normal musculo-skeletal development.

What is being proposed then is that movement experience in its widest sense is the basis on which later development of all kinds builds. It is responsible directly or indirectly for the building up of certain fundamental schemata (in Piaget's terms); cell assemblies and phase sequences (in Hebb's (1949) terms); analysers (in Deutsch's (1969) and Sutherland's (1959) terms); abilities (in Fleishman's (1967) terms) and sub-routines out of which complex movement patterns are later elaborated. What one must be aware of, is in attributing too much to movement per se for as Doll (1966) suggests, there is a hint that through some occult process transfer of training occurs with generalised educational improvement in non-motor areas. Most of the evidence which will be reviewed, unfortunately comes from the many *deprivation* studies which exist both in the animal and human sphere there being less evidence for precocious development as the result of for example an enriched and varied environment in terms of movement experience.

If we are really interested in early development, then clearly we are concerned with development post conception which includes the period intra-uterine. Evidence of the kind which may interest us is limited so we shall not dwell too long in this area. Paediatricians however and those concerned with preventative medicine might in this respect pay particular attention to the possible causes of brain damage etc which lead to forms of impairment (Section 5) which can affect later development.

In the main it would appear that the interest of the educationalist and the medical profession (at least until comparatively recent years) has been superficial. The effects of the intra-uterine environment on cognitive development have been largely ignored. The work of Stott (1966) and Knobloch and Pasamanick (1961) emphasises the possible importance of *stress* in pregnancy and birth complications on the development of an integrated nervous system. Rostand (1966) the French biologist has perhaps taken a further look into the future in this respect when he suggests:

> In the light of Konrad Lorenz's experiments—from which it has been

discovered that a bird's behaviour can be influenced in all its subsequent conduct by the first visual images that it received when it leaves the egg—it is inevitable that one should dream of the possibility of modifying the psyche by stimulation applied immediately after or even before birth. The human foetus has a sensory life: no one can foretell what effect might be produced by skilled prenatal 'education' whether it were produced by chemistry or by psycho-conditioning, intellectual superiority thus acquired would clearly not be transmissable to the descendant; the superiority treatment would have to be renewed in each generation.

Brave new world indeed!

As far as significance of movement in utero is concerned, little is firmly established but what is known is of interest and sufficient to indicate the importance of further research. Langreder (1949) (Quoted by Prechtl, 1966) for example suggests that movement of the foetus may be an active factor in its reaching and maintaining the vertex presentation during the last trimester of pregnancy. It is also significant in this respect that in cases of marked *motor abnormalities* of the foetus, abnormal intra-uterine positions occur much more frequently (Prechtl, 1966).

In view of what is widely accepted about the inability of unmyelinated nerve fibres to conduct impulses it must be assumed that such movements are reflex in action. This is not completely proven, neither is it known to what extent increasing the opportunity for movement in utero can aid the foetal position and hence the ease of the birth process and lessening of the risk of birth damage. Neither is it known to what extent such movement might contribute to the integrity of the nervous system. Evidence in this respect although often anecdotal is developing. Heyns (1963) in South Africa has initiated a procedure termed abdominal decompression which is a method of treatment designed to reduce the pressure in the abdomen of pregnant women particularly in the last trimester of pregnancy. Heyns in his earlier work, advocated the advantage of such a procedure in relieving the pain suffered in labour, in primary dysmenorrhoea and in simple backache. Some of the interest in his early work centred around the condition of the babies born to parents using this method during pregnancy. Many of these babies were shown to be superior in physical and mental development. Unfortunately, there were many methodological difficulties in this study and a follow-up by Liddicoat (1968) in which Heyns was involved found no support for such precocity. I mention the matter here, as I feel that there will be further developments in this area in subsequent years.

Heyns' interpretations of his findings (which included no cases of cerebral palsy) was in terms of increasing placental blood supply and the prevention of hypoxia during the first stages of labour, other findings have been the heightened activity of the foetus. The writer took up this topic with Heyns some years ago and in his reply he stated:

> Your point about the significance of movement for development I presume means physical foetal movement in utero. There cannot possibly by any writing on the matter, because obstetrics have so far seen only one side viz. that convulsive movements are dangerous and indicate imminent death. We have seen another side of the matter and regard it as an awakening perhaps of consciousness in the foetus.
>
> Our women have repeatedly said that they feel life more clearly after a run of D. One woman who had apparatus at home went off for an Easter weekend but could not take the equipment with her. When it came to the Monday or Tuesday she said to her husband that the baby must be sulking because of having missed out on D. This observation is seen repeatedly and I have no misgivings about its meaning. The foetus is in my view undoubtedly in better condition when it is active. It is not difficult to understand how when it is moribund it makes convulsive movements, because it is like a man being strangled.

An interpretation of why movement in utero might lead to precocious development must be approached with caution. Some writers (e.g. Feldenkrais, 1949; Zubeck and Solberg (1954), and Zagora, 1959) have drawn attention to the reciprocal influence of myelinisation and movement behaviour such that myelinisation plays a role in facilitating the onset of behaviour and behaviour serves to accelerate myelinisation rate but evidence of such a relationship is not well founded.

Again, this is only one of a number of possible explanations. Stress has already been suggested as a causal factor (Stott, 1966) in childhood impairment. It is possible that mothers undergoing Heyns' treatment do in consequence experience stress reduction both in a physical and mental sense. In this respect, attention is drawn to another series of African studies (Geber and Dean, 1957; Geber, 1960; 1961) which have shown similar precocious development in the absence of abdominal decompression or other artificial aids.

Movement and Perception

A number of workers in the field of child development give motivation for another line of approach to the problem of movement and early development which is worth elaborating. Hunt (1961) for example has attributed incidences of marked retardation in children to the homogeneity of 'input' during the early years. In a similar way, Fiske and Maddi (1961) suggest that it may be changes in perceptual input rather than opportunity for motor response that is most important in the motivation of psychological development. The point to stress here, is that in accepting the suggestions of both Hunt and Fiske and Maddi, one is not denying the importance of movement because one of the primary difficulties experienced in experimental attempts to support or refute such statements is that of isolating the contribution of the factors of sensory, perceptual and movement experience. They either interact or are confounded as experimental variables. In restricting opportunity for perceptual experience for example, it is generally necessary to restrict opportunity for movement. This is one of the problems implicit in interpreting the Schaffer studies reported in Section 6 (to which the reader is referred).

An attempt to assess the role of movement experience as against perceptual experience was made in two important animal studies. In a study of rats reared in small cages restricting body movement but not perception, Hymovitch (1952) showed that such animals performed much better in maze learning than comparable animals who had been reared in enclosed activity wheels (i.e. with minimal visual and auditory perceptual cues). Indeed, if the cages were moved from time to time, the rats did as well in perceptual tests as those brought up in a 'free' environment. Forgays and Forgays (1952) found their free movement group much superior to rats raised in mesh cages which *severely* limited movement experience. This, taken with the importance of distance cues for maze learning suggested by Hymovitch and supported experimentally by the Forgays, points to the conclusion that movement in space plays a real part in the development of visual function.

Although it is difficult to separate out the respective contributions of movement and perceptual deprivation, the fact that in the Hymovitch study, rats restricted in cages, but whose cages were moved about were indistinguishable from animals who had been free to move about in the environment leads to the suggestion that it is not movement restriction per se but the fact that the animals are being deprived of opportunity for varied perceptual experience. Voluntary movement is one means of varying perceptual input and moreover, the method usually employed. While this is one of the interpretations that might be put forward, it should be recalled that movement and proprioception are intimately related. Two interesting reports in relation to such an interpretation are provided by Bernhaut et al (1953) and Kulka et al (1960). The former workers for example maintain that kinesthetic stimuli are even more important than visual or auditory for reticular excitation. An activation/arousal concept of this nature was introduced in Section 1 and will be elaborated further in Section 6 in connection with the Schaffer studies already mentioned. Kulka and his co-workers have proposed that rocking and head banging and other such rhythmic movements which are seen in infants with prolonged deprivation may be an attempt to gratify their own kinesthetic needs i.e. to raise their abnormally low 'arousal' level.

The importance of movement in space for the development of perceptual abilities is further instanced in the studies of Held and his colleagues. They have shown that behavioural adjustments to rearranged visual fields (by use of distortion spectacles incorporating for example prism lenses) significantly improved when the individual was permitted to *voluntarily* initiate movement within the distorted environment. After extensive investigation of the phenomenon, these workers were led to the conclusion that the same mechanism was probably involved in the individual's adaptation to a rearranged visual field as was involved in the original acquisition of spatial behaviour by the child and that in either, case, movement with its concurrent feedback is a vital ingredient in the development of spatially coordinated behaviour. Held and Hein (1963) in a particularly neat experiment attempted to show the importance of reafferent information (feedback information from self-produced movement) on the integrity of the visual-perceptual mechanisms of kittens. Early deprivation of such self-produced movement in a structured environment appeared to adversely affect perceptual development.

The implication of the work of Held et al is that an *active* test is performed on the input. Some people (e.g. Festinger et al, 1967) have contended on the basis of such results that perception is in fact a 'motor' phenomenon although this would appear to be an extreme view. Such an idea has for example been criticised by Pribram (1971).

More recently, Gibson (1966) has elaborated his contention that the senses should be considered as perceptual systems and in so doing confirms some of the suggestions being made about the interrelationship between movement and perception. Gibson differentiates between *passive receptors* (the retina of the eye, the cochlea of the inner ear etc.) which respond to stimulus energy impinging upon them and *perceptual systems* which actively seek information. In these terms, the infant from birth (or even before) starts to select information from his environment. His perceptual systems (e.g. eye in head, head on body) cannot be exactly oriented at first and his attention is imprecise. Nevertheless, he voluntarily looks at things, touches and mouths them and listens to events. As he grows and develops psychologically, he learns to use his perceptual mechanisms more skilfully and his attention becomes educated to the subtleties of stimulus information (the skilful development of such orienting responses was discussed in Section 1). He does *learn* to perceive, but he does not have to learn to convert sense data into perception. With this kind of interpretation, it is clear that movement may not have so much an intrinsic value in development of perception as that of serving the purpose of getting the individual into the right situation in order to be able to select the appropriate information. Thus, one might think of gross movement as a means of getting a person into a particular position which is only to be reached by locomotion or at the other extreme, one might think of fine movement of the eyes in orienting towards particular parts of a display while maintaining a reasonably static postural orientation.

Movement and the development of 'Self'

A number of developmental psychologists have maintained that a child's early awareness of 'self' is based on active exploration of himself and his near space and on his reactions to objects around him. Although James (1890) contention that the new-born child experiences the world as a 'booming buzzing confusion' would be open to question, it is clear that a major function of early movement behaviour is that of developing a body-image—of learning to separate out 'self' from others. Early tactual experience with the mother together with auditory and visual experience and gross movements of the arms and legs serve as base-line information on which differentiation of bodily structure and function is based. While Kephart's (1960) suggestion that early tonic-neck reflex positions are the beginning of the establishment of laterality is debatable, it would seem apparent that the monitoring of movement (visually and kinesthetically) across the mid-line of the body would serve this function.

The infant's exploration of objects in his environment, of his own body and the bodies of others is the beginning of the development of a 'sense of self' as separate from the world around him. At the same time he begins to build up a spatial representation of his environment which will serve as a mediating mechanism in all his later skilled actions. The essential importance of this process and its effect on later development is elaborated by Bernstein (1967):

> Over the course of ontogenesis each encounter of a particular individual with the surrounding environment, with conditions requiring the solution of a motor problem, results in a development (sometimes a very valuable one), in its nervous system of increasingly reliable and accurate *objective representations* of the external world, both in terms of the perception and comprehension involved in meeting the situation, and in terms of projecting and controlling the realisation of the movements adequate to this situation. Each meaningful motor directive demands not an arbitrarily coded, but an objective, quantitatively and qualitatively reliable representation of the surrounding environment in the brain. Such an action is also an active implement for the correct cognition of the surrounding world. The achievement or failure of a solution to every active motor problem encountered during life leads to a progressive filtering and cross-indexing of the evidence in the sensory

syntheses mentioned above and in their components. This also leads to knowledge through action and *revision through practice* which is the cornerstone of the entire dialectical-materialistic theory of knowledge and in the cases selected here serves as a sort of biological context for Lenin's theory of reflection.

An original 'global' impression of the body gives rise not only to a cortical representation of the external environment, but to an awareness of the parts of the body, the way in which they interrelate in structure and function and their potential for displacement in the environment. That is, towards differentiation of inner structure and function and towards an appreciation of spatial concepts such as 'top and bottom', 'back and front', 'right and left' in relation to the body as a frame of reference (Whiting et al, 1974). A concept will be developed of the body as having definite limits or boundaries and of the parts within as being discrete yet interrelated (differentiation/integration hypothesis) and joined in a definite structure (Witkin et al, 1962).

Allport (1955) maintained that body-sense-coenaesthesis (proprioceptive information from viscera, muscles, tendons, joints, vestibular canals)—is not only one of the first categories of information to be encountered by the child in its developing awareness, but that:

> . . . it remains a life-long anchor for our self-awareness though it never accounts entirely for the sense of self.

Allport's position is supported more recently by Freedman (1961) in his contention that the body-schema requires continual maintenance by constant sampling of the environment. Head as long ago as 1926 maintained that each momentary experience is interpreted in relation to the moment to moment variations in one's *postural* experiences.

Conclusion

Consideration of the above comments—brief as they have been—should make the reader aware of the amount we take for granted in our movement behaviour. Many of the problems encountered when failures occur in the above systems manifest themselves in movement impairment which is discussed in the next section.

References

ALLPORT, G.H. (1955). *Theories of Perception and the Concept of Structure*. New York: Wiley.

ALSTON, W.P. (1974). Conceptual prolegomena to a psychological theory of intentional action. In S.C. Brown (Ed.) *Philosophy of Psychology*. London: Macmillan.

BERNHAUT, M., GELLHORN E. & RASMUSSEN, A.T. (1953). Experimental contributions to problems of consciousness. *J. Neurophysiol.*, **16**, 21-25.

BERNSTEIN, N. et al (1940). Studies of the biodynamics of walking, running and jumping. Researches of the Central Scientific Institute of Physical Culture, Moscow.

BERNSTEIN, N. (1967). *The Coordination and Regulation of Movements*. London: Pergamon.

BOWER, T.G.R. (1974). *Development in Infancy*. San Francisco: Freeman.

BROOKE, J.D. & WHITING, H.T.A. (1972). *Human Movement—a field of study*. London: Henry Kimpton.

CONNOLLY, K. (1969). The application of operant conditioning to the measurement development of motor skill in children. *Dev. Med. Child. Neurol.*, **10**, 697-705.

CONNOLLY, K. (1971). The evolution and ontogeny of behaviour. *Bull. Brit. Psychol. Soc.*, **24**, 93-102.

DEUTSCH, J.A. (1960). *The Structural Basis of Behaviour*. London: Cambridge University Press.

DOLL, E.A. (1966). SLD and motor training. *Percept. Motor Skills*, **23**, 220.

FELDENKRAIS, M. (1949). *Body and Mature Behaviour*. London: Routledge and Kegan Paul.

FESTINGER, L., BURNHAM, C.A., ONO, H. & BAMBER, D. (1967). Efference and the conscious experience. *J. Exp. Psychol.*, **74**, 1-36.

FISKE, D.W. & MADDI, S.R. (1961). *Functions of Varied Experience*. Illinois: Dorsey.

FLEISHMAN, E.A. (1967). Individual differences and motor learning. In R.M. Gagne (Ed.) *Learning and Individual Differences*. Ohio: Merrill.

FORGAYS, D.G. & FORGAYS, J.W. (1952). The nature of the effect of free environmental experience in the rat. *J. Comp. Physiol. Psychol.*, **45**, 322-328.

FREEDMAN, S.J. (1961). Sensory deprivation: facts in search of a theory *J. Nerv. Mental Dis.*, **132**, 17-21.

GEBER, M. & DEAN, R.F.A. (1957). Gessell tests on African children. *Pediatrics*, **20**, 51-57.

GEBER, M. (1958). The psychomotor development of African children in the first year and the influence of maternal behaviour. *J. Soc. Psychol.*, **47**, 185-195.

GEBER, M. (1961). Longitudinal study and psychomotor development among African children. Proceedings of the XIVth International Congress of Applied Psychology, Copenhagen.

GIBSON, J.J. (1966). *The Senses Considered as Perceptual Systems.* London: George Allen & Unwin.

HEAD, H. (1926). *Aphasia and Kindred Disorders of Speech.* London: Cambridge University Press.

HEBB, D.O. (1949). *The Organisation of Behaviour.* New York: Wiley.

HEBB, D.O. (1966). Drives and the C.N.S. (conceptual nervous system). *Psychol. Rev.,* **62**, 243-254.

HELD, R. & HEIN, A. (1963). Movement produced stimulation in the development of visually guided behaviour. *J. Comp. Physiol. Psychol.,* **56**, 872-874.

HEYNS, O.S. (1963). *Abdominal Decompression.* Johannesburgh: Witwatersrand University Press.

HUNT, J. McV. (1961). *Intelligence and Experience.* New York: Ronald Press.

HUTT, C. (1974). Critique of 'Direct observation' by Cooper et al. *Bull. Brit. Psychol. Soc.,* **27**, 503-504.

HYMOVICH, B. (1952). The effects of experimental variations on problem solving in the rat. *J. Comp. Psychol.,* **45**, 313-320.

JAMES, W. (1890). *Principles of Psychology.* London: Macmillan.

KEPHART, N.C. (1960). *The Slow-learner in the Classroom.* Ohio: Merrill.

KNOBLOCH, H. & PASAMANICK, B. (1961). *Prevention of Mental Disorders in Children.* New York: Basic Books.

KULKA, A., FRY, C. & GOLDSTEIN, F.J. (1960). Kinesthetic needs in infancy. *Am. J. Orthopsychiat.,* **30**, 306-314.

LANGREDER, W. (1949). Uber fotal reflexe und deren intrauterine Bedeutung. *Z. Gerburtsh. Gynak.,* **131**, 237-252.

LEVINE, S. & MULLINS, R.F. (1966). Hormonal influences on brain organisation in infant rats. *Science,* **152**, 1585-1592.

LIDDICOAT, R. (1968). The effects of maternal antenatal decompression treatment on infant mental development. *S. Afr. Med. J.,* March 2nd.

PIAGET, J. (1955). *The Child's Construction of Reality.* London: Routledge & Kegan Paul.

PRECHTL, H. (Ed.) (1966). *Advances in the Study of Child Behaviour II.* New York: Academic Press.

PRIBRAM, K.H. (1971). *Languages of the Brain.* New Jersey: Prentice-Hall.

ROBERTS, E. & MATTHYSSE, S. (1970). Neurochemistry: at the crossroads of neurobiology. *Ann. Rev. Biochem.,* **39**, 777-820.

ROSTAND, J. (1966). The future of biology. In J. Rostand & A. Delaunay (Directors) *The Living Universe: an encyclopaedia of the biological sciences.* London: Nelson.

SHERRINGTON, C.S. (1951). *Man on his Nature.* Cambridge: University Press.

STOTT, D.H. (1966). A general test of motor impairment for children. *Dev. Med. Child Neur.,* **8**, 523-531.

SUTHERLAND, N.S. (1959). Stimulus analysing mechanisms. In *Proceedings of a Symposium on the Mechanisation of Thought Processes. Vol. II,* 575-609. London: H.M.S.O.

WELTON, J. (1912). *The Psychology of Education.* London: Macmillan.

WHITING, H.T.A., HARDMAN, K., HENDRY, L.B. & JONES, M.G. (1974). *Personality and Performance in Physical Education and Sport.* London: Henry Kimpton.

WITKIN, H.A., DYK, R.B., FATERSON, H.F., GOODENOUGH, D.R. & KARP, S.A. (1962). *Psychological Differentiation.* New York: Wiley.

ZAGORA, E. (1959). Observations on the evolution and neurophysiology of eye-limb coordination. *Opthalmologica,* **138**, 242-254.

ZUBECK, J.P. & SOLBERG, P.A. (1954). *Human Development.* London: McGraw-Hill.

5

MOTOR IMPAIRMENT – AN OVERVIEW

5 MOTOR IMPAIRMENT– AN OVERVIEW

Most of the work carried out in skill acquisition has been concerned with an analysis of the performance of highly skilled operators. There is however another end to the continuum, that of the relatively unskilled. An examination of concepts related to such impairment can provide illuminating information on the acquisition of skill in general.

Motor impairment is a sub-classification of the wider domain—movement impairment. The latter concept is concerned with the inadequacy of an individual's *physical* responses to the everyday demands of his environment. It is a condition which manifests itself in performances which are subnormal or whose efficiency has been grossly impaired (Whiting, 1972a). These performances reflect inadequate attempts to perform those motor skills which can be regarded either as being essential for a normal life or at the least, culturally desirable (Morris and Whiting, 1971). An *impairment continuum* might be proposed ranging from *gross* impairments at the one extreme—which necessitate clinical recognition and treatment—to those *apparently* minor forms of impairment at the other which might appropriately be classified as manifesting 'clumsiness' and which in consequence are often accepted as 'within the norm'. Considerable medical interest has of necessity been directed to the more gross forms of impairment, but, until comparatively recent years, the 'clumsy child' had received little formal attention or experimental investigation. While gross forms of impairment such as ataxia, chorea, hemiplegia, spasticity etc. must remain a clinical diagnostic and treatment problem, an understanding of the nature of such impairments and a concern for rehabilitation and compensatory education procedures may well fall within the bounds of interest of the human movement specialist.

The fact that motor impairment (clumsiness) has received more detailed attention from educationists and psychologists rather than from the medical profession, is perhaps not surprising. To some extent, this has been brought about by postulated links between such forms of impairment and intellectual and social development (Morris and Whiting, 1971).

91

The concept of motor impairment

The concept of motor impairment (Stott's 1966 clumsiness syndrome) is a difficult one to elaborate. Stott (1966) for example has defined motor impairment as:

> . . . that which constitutes any dysfunction in the everyday activities of the child.

What is implied here, is a failure to make the necessary physical adjustments to the environment *in which he finds himself.* Since children occupy different social milieu it is obvious that what is accepted as 'within the norm' in one environment will be taken as *abnormal* within another. This was brought out forcibly in a recent investigation carried out at Leeds across schools with widely differing social conditions. When for example a child from what is normally recognised as a good social area was considered to be impaired, he might be extremely able when compared with children from the very poor social areas. A unitary concept of impairment does not exist, it is like skill a relative term. This does of course impose difficulties if it is wished to bring together children from widely differing social backgrounds for the purpose of compensatory education and also raises problems as to the criteria to be adopted for the institution of compensatory education procedures.

The absence of firmly established criteria of motor impairment also poses problems related to the establishment of tests for its assessment. This is reflected in the necessity to adopt arbitrary criteria in the most recently developed test by Stott, Moyes and Headridge (Stott, 1966).

While the problems raised mainly relate to the question of objectivity and the establishment of criteria for assessment and compensatory education, at a subjective level the concept is well recognised. Many parents have little difficulty in operationally defining the syndrome and in being aware of the fact that these children are abnormal.

The following abstracts taken at random from recent letters to the writer support this contention and at the same time, provide interesting case material:

1 My son, eleven years of age, has very poor co-ordination. This was first noticed when he was learning to walk which he began to do about 10 and a half months of age. He was unsteady in balancing himself. As he grew older, we noticed that he stumbled frequently, and in fighting with other boys, his punches never seemed to land where he aimed. This has been a definite handicap to him because since he is poor in defending himself he is constantly on the defensive. Athletically he is 'scorned' by boys his own age. This has

also been a handicap He suffers socially with children who are aware of his handicap.

2 This account would seem to describe my son who is 5½ years old. His poor co-ordination has affected him socially for at least the last two years. A year ago I took him for a check up at the local cerebral palsy clinic which is all there is available in this area. The doctor didn't even examine him and only casually watched him walk in and then said he was perfectly normal in all respects.

Granted he is within 'normal' limits! However, there has always been 'something slightly off'. He falls constantly without being aware of why—small muscle co-ordination is poor—it's difficult for him to hold a pencil.

Motor impairment—a misnomer

The use of the term 'motor' in the phrase *motor impairment* while being useful as a descriptive term is limiting when explanations of such impairment are being sought. While *human* skill learning and performance is concerned with *intentional* attempts to carry out motor acts, which will bring about predetermined end results, it is clear that such acts are the resultant of a whole chain of processes which affect their outcome. Thus, the deficiency implicit in the term *motor* impairment may lie in one or more parts of a whole network of processes involved in the input of information to the system, decision-making on the basis of such information and the formulating of an executive response. For this reason, a more acceptable and descriptive term would be *perceptual-motor impairment* which draws attention to the important relationship which exists between the input and output sides of performance. Such an analysis becomes even more understandable if an information-processing model of skilled performance is adopted (Welford, 1968; Whiting, 1969; Morris and Whiting, 1971; Whiting, 1972b).

A model of the kind proposed, treats the human organism as an information-processing system in which the primary subsystems are concerned with the reception of information (sense organs); the organisation and interpretation of such information (perceptual mechanisms); decision-making on the basis of such information (translatory mechanisms) and the initiation of a motor response (effector mechanisms). Such a model can be applied to the acquisition and performance of all kinds of skills (verbal, motor, social and intellectual) and it is likely that a deficiency in any of the subsystems will affect the outcome of a wide range of such skills. Such deficits may be structural (e.g. brain damage) or functional (e.g. a failure to establish appropriate mediating mechanisms (Morris and Whiting, 1971).

This kind of model has already proved its heuristic value and focussed attention on the interaction between the organism and environment involved in any skilled behaviour.

Workers in the field of compensatory education are beginning to appreciate many of the ideas implicit in the above analysis and to formulate their procedures on this kind of basis (e.g. Ayres, 1963; Argy, 1965; Frostig, 1968; Hart, 1970; Kamii and Radin, 1967).

Aetiology of motor impairment

The primary aetiological considerations under this heading are those with neurological involvement. On a broad basis, these can be categorised as *brain damage* and *brain dysfunction* with an appreciation that the two are obviously related. The impaired perceptual-motor performances observed in *known* cases of brain-damage has in the past led investigators to generalise to other instances of perceptual-motor impairment where brain damage is less obvious.

Brain damage *per se,* represents a structural change brought about by physical causes, haemorrhage, toxic reactions and anoxia. However, a failure to detect signs of organic damage does not necessarily imply the absence of what has been termed *brain dysfunction.* The implication here, is of a cerebral disorganisation in a neurophysiological rather than a neuroanatomical sense. This concept has been discussed in the context of impairment by Morris and Whiting (1971); Clarke (1966); Stott (1966); Gubbay et al (1965); Walton et al (1962); Fish (1961) and Ford (1959).

A deficiency in skilled behaviour, may be the result of a *breakdown* in already established skill performance, or an inherent inability to carry out successfully the skill which is demanded, at a sufficiently adaptive level. Although major emphasis in this context will centre around the latter category, it should be borne in mind that temporary breakdowns can be brought about by toxic influences such as alcohol, drugs and mystical experience which may become permanent deficits if such behaviour persists. The aetiology of such inherent disabilities centres around genetic predisposition, brain-damage, an impoverished environment or combinations of two or more of these factors. Such aetiological considerations can best be illustrated by focussing attention on prenatal, paranatal and postnatal factors. (These have been developed in detail by Morris and Whiting (1971)):

    (a) Prenatal factors—the resultant of genetic influences, injurious conditions in utero or combinations of the two. Amongst the major factors in this respect are:

        prenatal anoxia, virus infection, rhesus factor, toxaemias of pregnancy, cigarette smoking, emotional disturbance

(b) Paranatal factors—premature birth, placenta praevia, precipitate labour, pelvic deformity, anomalies in presentation, forceps delivery, caesarian section, twin pregnancies.

(c) Postnatal factors—sensory, perceptual and movement deprivation. Although some workers discuss maternal deprivation as a separate category, it is likely that this can be reduced to sensory/perceptual deprivation (see Schaffer, 1965, 1966; Schaffer and Emerson, 1968 for possible reasons). It is clear from examination of evidence from some of the more extreme studies, that gross deprivation of one kind or another can result in impaired performance which at some later stage may give rise to maladaptive behaviour. Useful studies in this area have been reviewed by Newton and Levine (1968) and Schutz (1965).

Social class—the higher incidence of impairment of all kinds amongst children whose parents are classified in the lower social classes leads to a consideration of the factors which might be operating in such a social setting (Fairweather and Illsley, 1960).

Specific/generality of motor impairment

Children who may be unable to perform a *particular* skill are not automatically incapable of acquiring other skills where different abilities are involved. The hand-eye co-ordination of movements required to catch a ball may present difficulties to a child who, because for example of a visual defect, is unable to monitor the flight of the ball adequately. The same child might be extremely proficient in throwing a ball to hit a stationary target. Some children who show a high degree of co-ordination and skill on the games field may have difficulty in performing the finer movements involved in handwriting.

It is also evident, that at the other end of the motor impairment continuum, more global and far reaching effects may be present limiting the child's possibility of performing a wide variety of motor skills. When such severe impairment exists, it seems probable that it may be accompanied by and be the cause of disturbances in other aspects of human performance. Fish (1961) for example noted that in children of school age a derangement of motor and perceptual functions tended to be associated with an interference in the intellectual functioning when the disturbance was sufficiently severe. While the relationship between motor and mental performance has always been the subject of dispute and conflicting evidence, there would appear to be more agreement amongst workers in this field of a significant positive relationship if the complete range of mental ability is taken into account. Mentally retarded subjects in the main would appear to demonstrate less motor competence (Malpass, 1971; Fish, 1961; Sloan, 1948; Whiting et al, 1969).

Possible links between behaviour disorders and motor impairment have been suggested by Knobloch and Pasamanick (1959); Pasamanick et al (1956); Rogers et al (1955) and Corah et al (1965). Interpretation of why such a linkage should exist may be made by consideration such as:

(a) A 'general' inability to acquire skill which affects social as well as other skills because of damage to or dysfunction in the subsystems concerned with perceptual motor skill performance.

(b) The interaction between mother and infant which results in tension patterns in the mother (Barker and Wright, 1955; Richardson 1964; Fairweather and Illsley, 1960; Casler, 1968; Prechtl, 1963; Stott, 1962; Hewett et al, 1970).

(c) The 'status significance' that competence in physical skills carries at particular stages of childhood and the effect this might have on the development of the individual's self-esteem (Morris and Whiting, 1971; Hewett et al, 1970; Jones and Bayley, 1950).

Stott (1959; 1962; 1964) perhaps more than any other worker has linked motor impairment with maladjustment and delinquency. He hypothesises a factor of congenital impairment. Support for this proposition comes from the work of Whiting et al (1970); Drillien (1964); Prechtl (1961); Bamber (1966).

The 'ability' concept

The specificity/generality problem posed above can be appreciated by a consideration of the 'ability' concept as suggested in Section 3. Fleishman (1967) makes a useful distinction between 'ability' and 'skill'. The latter referring to the level of proficiency in a specific task or limited group of tasks. Abilities enter into and are necessary for the performance of skills. Certain abilities are more basic in the sense that they are related to performance on diverse tasks. The implication of this dichotomy, is that the level of skilled performance depends upon abilities which are present before embarking on the task. Furthermore, Fleishman maintains that certain abilities are task specific and thus can only be acquired within that skill. Transfer of training across skills on this basis would be determined by the extent to which they required similar abilities for their performance.

The idea that basic abilities place limits on later skill proficiency, is of fundamental importance in relation to motor, intellectual and social performance (Morris and Whiting, 1971). If in fact, brain-damage is present, or children have undergone sensory/perceptual deprivation, movement deprivation or combinations of these, it might reasonably be supposed that the possibility of their developing the appropriate abilities to a normal level, will be severely restricted and subsequent skilled behaviour, adversely affected.

The body-concept and motor impairment

The relationship between a relatively unsophisticated body-concept and motor-impairment is implicit in the attempts made by those concerned with compensatory education in this sphere to provide opportunities for enhancement of the body-concept. Problems with terminology make this a difficult field to evaluate. Thus, some workers use the term *Body-schema* (Schilder, 1935; Freedman, 1961; Piaget, 1952; Fisher, 1966), others related terminology such as:

> *Body-image* (Fenichel, 1945; Ritchie-Russell, 1958; Fisher and Cleveland, 1958; Wright, 1960; McKellar, 1965; Dibiase and Hjelle, 1968)
> *Body-awareness* (Morison, 1969)
> *Body-concept* (Witkin et al, 1962; Frostig and Horne, 1964)
> *Body-sense* (Allport, 1955)
> *Body-experience* (Jourard, 1967)

Moreover, while there is a degree of overlap in such varying concepts, they are by no means clearly defined. In the present context, the following operational definition (Benyon, 1968) of a defective body-concept is perhaps more useful:

> Each child was 'insecure' with himself; he was not aware of what, where or who he was or exactly how he was functioning with relation to his environment. His body often baffled him as it got him into constant trouble by bumping into things, tripping over itself, getting 'lost' in clothing, and failing to allow him to ride bikes, climb trees or play ball like any of his friends. He also found himself forgetting about his body often acting on impulse with total disregard for the consequences.

The limitations in such a definition are reflected in the primary emphasis on the output malfunctioning to the neglect of the cognitive and affective components of body-concept.

In terms of the development of the body-concept, it will be appreciated, that an original 'global' impression of the body gives way to an awareness of parts of the body, the way in which they interrelate in structure and function and their potential for displacement, within the environment. That is, in Witkin et al's (1962) terms towards *differentiation* of inner structure and function and towards an appreciation of spatial concepts (Whiting et al, 1972). The progress in ontological development is from a relatively field-dependent (Witkin et al, 1962) made of perceiving to a relatively field-independent mode which is paralleled by progress towards a more sophisticated body-concept. Witkin (1967) has produced some evidence that differences in the global-articulated style dimension reflect differences in socialisation procedures.

Kephart (1960) has been particularly active in recognising the relationship between development of the body-image and compensatory education procedures. He has emphasised the relationship between development of body-image, lateral and directional awareness and perceptual feedback in learning disabilities. Hill et al (1967) in an investigation into the effect of a systematic programme of exercises on the development of retarded children's awareness of right-left directionality, propose that programmes for training retarded children should include activities which give them many experiences in orientating their attention to the position of their own bodies in space relative to that of other objects as well as directing children to make responses with specified body parts. Similar procedures are recognised by Tansley (1967); Stephenson and Robertson (1965) and Frostig and Horne (1964).

The application of compensatory education to the development of the body-concept is not a particularly new idea. It was implicit in the early work of Schilder (1935) and Alexander (1957). Other useful work in this area has been carried out by Painter (1964); Holden (1962); Hobbs (1960). Useful overviews have been provided by Morris and Whiting (1971) and by Whiting et al, 1974:

Assessment of motor impairment

The problem of the assessment of motor impairment has already been referred to. The arbitrary nature of the cut-off point to be adopted makes development in this area particularly difficult. A postulated link between brain-damage and motor-impairment has in the past led to the conclusion that a test of brain-damage would be the most appropriate means of diagnosis. While such tests might be useful procedures with reasonably gross impairments, it is doubtful if they are sufficiently sensitive for cases of minimal motor impairment which can be attributed to brain damage. Consequently, a number of procedures have tended to be used either independently or together in an attempt to screen off those children requiring compensatory education. Amongst the more obvious ones are:

(i) Teacher/parent assessments after observation of motor performances. School records/intelligence tests/medical histories/home environment.

(ii) Medical examination—physical, neurological, electroencephalograph examination, motor impersistence tests (Garfield, 1964; Fisher, 1956; Joynt, Benton and Fogel, 1962; Prechtl and Stemmer, 1962; Rutter et al, 1966).

(iii) Specifically designed motor ability tests:

    (a)   Oseretzky tests (1923; 1929)

    (b)   Yarmolenko's Test (1933)

    (c)   Lincoln/Oseretzky revision (Sloan, 1955)

    (d)   Vineland adaptation of the Oseretzky test (Cassell, 1949)

    (e)   General test of motor impairment (Stott, 1966)

(iv) Psychometric tests:

    (a)   Tests used to identify brain-damage e.g. Bender-Gestalt test—Koppitz (1958); Pascal and Suttell (1957); Thweatt (1963); Miller et al (1963).
Memory for Designs Test—Graham and Kendall (1960); Garrett, Price and Deabler (1957); Clarke et al (1968).

    (b)   Tests of body-concept—Witkin et al (1962)

    (c)   Tests of specific factors of motor performance e.g. manual dexterity, speed/accuracy trade-off—spiral-maze test (Gibson 1964; Whiting et al 1969).

    (d)   Intelligence tests e.g. Wechsler (1949) intelligence test for children

    (e)   Tests of perceptual abilities e.g. developmental tests of visual perception (Frostig et al, 1961; Frostig, 1963).

Motor impairment and compensatory education

A deficiency in skilled behaviour (motor impairment) may be the result of:

1 A breakdown in already established skill performance
2 An inherent inability to carry out successfully the skill which is demanded

It is meaningful to talk about re-education in the first instance since the child once had the ability to perform the skill. With the child who has never been able to perform these particular skills efficiently, it is meaningless to talk about re-education, because in this sense they have not been educated!

The more useful term is compensatory education—additional or special education designed to compensate either for early deprivation or for the child's inability to deal with information in a meaningful way. It would for example be appropriate to refer to the various Head-start programmes for deprived children, as a form of compensatory education. (These essentially consist of taking pre-school children out of their impoverished homes for short periods and subjecting them to new experiences and especially to those experiences, objects and people they are likely to meet again when they commence school). Implicit in the concept of compensatory education is that deficient early experience can be compensated. This is a *necessary* act of faith on the part of any worker in this field.

It is interesting to note in relation to Head-start programmes that Pettigrew et al (1967) in an exhaustive report to the U.S. Commission on Civil Rights state:

> Tentative analyses of these programs have suggested that they have been initially successful but that much of the benefit has been lost when children have entered the regular grades of the public school system.

This does not necessarily mean that such compensatory education procedures are wrong in principle, but it does suggest that current methods of approach may not be the most beneficial. This raises an interesting problem. What in fact does determine the way in which compensatory education programme is set up? What criteria are adopted? Is there a logical development based on experimental findings or is it just a hit and miss procedure? To a large extent, the latter would appear to be the case but it is interesting to note recent developments in which workers have attempted to base their compensatory education procedures on realistic principles. Kamii and Radin (1967) for example have recently proposed a framework for pre-school curriculum based on some Piagetian concepts with particular emphasis on the sensori-motor stage.

On a broad basis, one's general philosophy of education reflects one's attitude to compensatory education programmes. If one accepts for example that brain damage where it exists is not only irreversible but can be compensated for by activities in other parts of the brain, then one might not be inclined to change one's method of approach but one might assume that the child is incapable of being helped. In the not too distant past, this has often been the case, and in some places still exists. Again, if one adopts a purely maturational viewpoint, one is conditioned to expecting an unfolding of innately determined patterns of development. Connolly (1968) makes a very salient point in this respect, in suggesting that failure or great difficulty on the part of a child to learn a given response has frequently been accounted for in terms of the child's not being ready or not being able to learn the response at the time whereas more concern should be centred around the efficiency of the teaching techniques adopted.

Kohlberg (1968) has recently elaborated three broad streams of educational thought:

1 Maturational stream. What is most important in the development of the child is that which comes from within i.e. the pedagogical environment should be one which creates a climate to allow inner abilities and social virtues to unfold and the inner bad to come under the control of the inner good—an emphasis on innate patterning and maturation.

2 Cultural training stream. The learning of the cognitive and moral knowledge and rules of the culture should be taught by direct instruction. An environmental-associationist approach.

3 Cognitive-developmental. The interactionist viewpoint which proposes that the cognitive and affective structures which education should nourish are natural emergents from the interaction between the child and the environment under conditions where such interaction is allowed for and fostered.

It would appear that those committed to compensatory education in its broadest sense must align themselves with the third approach. The primary emphasis then becomes *experience* in determining the extent of both cognitive and motor development. This is brought about by building up the mediating mechanisms between the environmental demands and the child's actions. The development of systems of internal relations, structures, rules for processing information or connecting experienced events. In summary, such an interactional interpretation assumes that experience is necessary for the developmental stages to take the shape they do as well as assuming that generally more or richer stimulation will lead to faster advances through the stages involved.

On a broad basis, compensatory education, procedures currently being used in relation to motor impairment can be classified as *Direct* (in which more stereotyped movement patterns are practised by the retardates— Kephart (1960); Oliver (1955, 1963); Oliver and Keogh (1967, 1968); Cratty (1969)) and *Indirect* (freedom for experimenting with a wide range of movement patterns—Tansley and Gulliford (1960); Argy (1965); Sherborne (1965); Bruce (1969)).

Other workers, have based their compensatory education procedures upon the recapitulation of developmental sequences—Tansley and Gulliford (1960); Kephart (1960); Cruickshank et al (1961); Sutphin (1964); Gallagher (1964); Ausubel (1967); Kamii and Radin (1967); Wedell (1964).

A further procedure has been to pay particular attention to particular characteristics of the syndrome:

Distractability—Gessell & Amatrude (1941); Floyer (1955); Cruickshank & Dolphin (1951); Francis-Williams (1964); Cratty (1969).

Disinhibition—Strauss & Kephart (1955); Cruickshank et al (1961)

Perserveration—Werner (1941); Strauss & Lehtinen (1948); Cardwell (1956); Tansley & Gulliford (1962); Cratty (1969).

Perceptual-motor functions—Strauss & Lehtinen (1948); Frostig (1961; 1963); Cratty (1969).

Development of body-awareness—Kephart (1960); Frostig & Horne (1966); Jakeman (1967); Frostig (1968); Cratty (1969).

Visual perception—Frostig (1961; 1963); Cratty (1969).

References

ALEXANDER, F.M. (1957). *The use of the self.* London: Re-educational Publicat.

ALLPORT, G.W. (1955). *Becoming.* New Haven: Yale Univ. Press.

ARGY, W.P. (1965). Montessori versus orthodox. *Rehabilitation Literature,* **26**, 10.

AYRES, A.J. (1963). The development of perceptual motor abilities: a theoretical basis for the treatment of dysfunction. *Amer. J. Occup. Therapy,* **17**, 221-225.

AUSUBEL, D.P. (1967). How reversible are the cognitive and maturational effects of cultural deprivation? In A.H. PASSOW, M. GOLDBERG, & A.J. TANNEBAUM (Eds.) *Education of the Disadvantaged.* New York: Holt, Rinehart and Winston.

BAMBER, J. (1966). Motor impairment & delinquency. Unpublished M.A. thesis. University of Glasgow.

BARKER, R.G. & WRIGHT, H.F. (1955). *Midwest and Its Children: the psychological ecology of an American town.* New York: Row and Peterson.

BENYON, S.D. (1968). *Intensive Programming for Slow Learners.* Ohio: Merrill.

BRUCE, V.R. (1969). *Awakening the Slow Mind.* London: Pergamon.

CARDWELL, V.E. (1956). *Cerebral Palsy: advances in understanding and care.* New York: North River Press.

CASLER, L. (1968). Perceptual deprivation in institutional settings. In G. Newton & S. Levine (Eds.) *Early Experience and Behaviour.* Springfield: Thomas.

CASSELL, R. (1949). Vineland adaption of the Oseretsky Tests. *Training School Bulletin* Supp. Vol. 43, 3-4.

CLARKE, P.R.F. (1966). The nature and consequences of brain lesions in children and adults. Proceedings of a course held by the English division of professional psychologists. London: British Psychological Society.

CLARKE, T.A., JOHNSON, G.A., MORRIS, P.R. & PAGE, M. (1968). Motor impairment: a study of clumsy children. Unpublished dissertation, Institute of Education, University of Leeds.

CONNOLLY, K. (1969). The application of operant conditioning to the measurement and development of motor skill in children. *Dev. Med. Child Neur.,* **10**, 697-705.

CORAH, N.L., ANTHONY, E.J., PAINTER, P., STERN, J.A., & THURSTON, D.L. (1965). Effects of perinatal anoxia after seven years. *Psych. Monog.,* **79**, 3, 1-33.

CRATTY, B.J. (1969). *Motor Activity and the Education of Retardates.* Philadelphia: Lea & Febiger.

CRUICKSHANK, W.M. & DOLPHIN, J.E. (1951). Educational implications of psychological studies of cerebral palsied children. *Except. Child.,* **18**, 1-8.

CRUICKSHANK, W.M., BENTZEN, F.A., RATZEBURG, F.H. & TANNHAUSER, M.T., (1961). *A Teaching Method for Brain Injured and Hyperactive Children.* Syracuse: University Press.

DIBIASE, W.J. & HJELLE, L.A. (1968). Body-image stereotypes and body-type preferences among male college students. *Percept. Motor Skills,* **27**, 1143-1146.

DRILLIEN, C.N. (1964). *Growth and Development of Prematurely Born Infants.* Edinburgh: Livingstone.

FAIRWEATHER, D.V. & ILLSLEY, R. (1960). Obstetric and social origins of mentally handicapped children. *Brit. J. Prev. Soc. Med.,* **14**, 149-159.

FENICHEL, O. (1945). *The Psychoanalytic Theory of Neurosis.* New York: Norton.

FISH, B. (1961). The study of motor development in infancy and its relation to psychological functioning. *Amer. J. Psychiat.,* **17**, 1113-1118.

FISHER, M. (1956). Left hemiplegia and motor impersistence. *J. Nerv. Ment. Dis.,* **123**, 201-218.

FISHER, S. (1966). Body attention patterns and personality defences. *Psych. Monogr.,* **80**, 9.

FISHER, S. & CLEVELAND, R.L. (1958). *Body-image and Personality.* Princeton: Van Nostrand.

FLEISHMAN, E.A. (1967). Individual differences and motor learning. In R.M. Gagne (Ed.) *Individual Differences.* Ohio: Merrill.

FLOYER, E.B. (1955). *A Psychological Study of a City's Cerebral Palsied Children.* London: Brit. Council Welfare of Spastics.

FORD, F.R. (1959). *Diseases of the Nervous System in Infancy, Childhood and Adolescence.* Springfield: Thomas.

FREEDMAN, S.J. (1961). Sensory deprivation: facts in search of a theory. *J. Nerv. Ment. Dis.,* **132**, 17-21.

FRANCES-WILLIAMS, J. (1964). *Understanding and Helping the Distractible Child.* London: Spastics Society.

FROSTIG, M., LEFEVER, D.W. & WHITTLESEY, D.R.B. (1961). A developmental test of visual perception for everyday normal and neurologically handicapped children. *Percept. Motor Skills,* **12**, 383-389.

FROSTIG, M. (1963). *Developmental Test of Visual Perception.* California: Consulting Psychologists' Press.

FROSTIG, M. & HORNE, D. (1964). *The Frostig Program for the Development of Visual Perception.* Chicago: Follet.

FROSTIG, M. (1968). Sensory-motor development. *Special Education,* **57**, 2, 18-20.

GALLAGHER, J.J. (1964). *The Tutoring of Brain-injured Mentally Retarded Children.* Springfield: Thomas.

GARFIELD, J.C. (1964). Motor impersistence in normal and brain-damaged children. *Neurology,* **14**, 623-630.

GARRETT, E.S., PRICE, A.C. & DEABLER, H.L. (1957). Diagnostic testing for cortical brain impairment. *Arch. Neurol. Psychiat.,* **77**, 223-225.

GESELL, A. & AMATRUDE, C.S. (1941). *Developmental Diagnosis.* New York: Hoeber.

GIBSON, H.B. (1964). The spiral maze: a psychomotor test with implications for the study of delinquency. *Brit. J. Psych.,* **54**, 219-225.

GRAHAM, F.A. & KENDALL, S. (1960). Memory for designs. *Percept. Motor Skills,* **11**, 147-188.

GUBBAY, S.S., ELLIS, E., WALTON, J.N. & COURT, S.D.M. (1965). A study of apraxic and agnosic defects in 21 children. *J. Neur.,* **88**.

HART, R.L.A. (1970). Perceptual deficiency. *Forward Trends,* Feb., 19-20.

HEWETT, S., NEWSON, J. & NEWSON, E. (1970). *The Family and the Handicapped Child.* London: Allen & Unwin.

HILL, S.D. et al (1967). Relation of training in motor activity to development of right-left directionality in mentally-retarded children. *Percept. Motor Skills,* **24**, 363-366.

HOBBS, N. (1966). Helping disturbed children's psychological and ecological strategies. *Amer. Psychol.,* **21**, 1105-1115.

HOLDEN, R.H. (1962). Changes in the body-image of physically handicapped children due to summer day camp experience. *Merrill Palmer Quart.*, 8, 19-26.

JAKEMAN, D. (1967). The Marianne Frostig approach. *Forward Trends*, 11, 3, 99-100.

JONES, M.C. & BAYLEY, N. (1950). Physical maturing among boys related to behaviour. *J. Educ. Psych.*, 41, 129-148.

JOURARD, S. (1967). Out of touch–body-taboo. *New Society*, 9.

JOYNT, R.J., BENTON, A.L. & FOGEL, M.L. (1962). Behavioural and pathological correlation of motor impersistence. *Neurology*, 12, 876-881.

KAMII, C.K. & RADIN, N.L. (1967). A framework for a pre-school curriculum based on some Piagetian concepts. *J. Creative Behaviour*, 1, 3, 314-323.

KEPHART, N.C. (1960). *The Slow-learner in the Classroom.* Ohio: Merrill.

KNOBLOCH, H. & PASAMANICK, B. (1959). Geographic and seasonal variation in birth rates. *Pub. Health Report* (U.S.A.) 74, 4, 285-289.

KOHLBERG, L. (1968). Early education: a cognitive-developmental view. *Child Development*, 39 (4), 1013-1062.

KOPPITZ, E.M. (1958). The Bender Gestalt Test and learning disturbances in young children. *J. Clin. Psych.*, 14, 292-295.

MALPASS, L.F. (1961). Motor skills in mental deficiency. In E. Ellis (Ed.) *Handbook of Mental Deficiency.* New York: McGraw-Hill.

MCKELLAR, P. (1965). Thinking, remembering and imagining. In J.G. Howells (Ed.) *Modern Perspectives in Child Psychiatry.* Edinburgh: Oliver & Boyd.

MILLER, L.C., LOWENFELD, R., LINDER, R. & TURNER, J. (1963). Reliability of Kopptiz' scoring system for the Bender Gestalt. *J. Clin. Psych.*, 19, 2111.

MORISON, R. (1969). *A Movement Approach to Educational Gymnastics.* London: Dent.

MORRIS, P.R. & WHITING, H.T.A. (1971). *Motor Impairment and Compensatory Education.* Philadelphia: Lea & Febiger. London: Bell.

NEWTON, G. & LEVINE, S. (Eds.) (1968). *Early Experience and Behaviour.* Springfield: Thomas.

OLIVER, J.N. (1955). Physical education for educationally sub-normal children. *Educat. Rev.*, 8, 122-136.

OLIVER, J.N. (1963). The physical education of E.S.N. children. *Forward Trends*, 7, 3, 87-90.

OLIVER, J.N. & KEOGH, J.F. (1967). Helping the physically awkward. *Special Education*, 56, 22-26.

OLIVER, J.N. & KEOGH, J.F. (1968). A clinical study of physically awkward E.S.N. boys. *Res. Quart.*, 39, 301-307.

OSERETSKY, N. (1923). Metric scale for studying the motor capacity of children. Published in Russian. Referred to in Rudolph Lassner, Annotated bibliography of the Oseretsky test of motor proficiency. *J. Consult. Psych.*, 1948, 12, 37-47.

OSERETSKY, N. (1929). A group method of examining the motor functions of children and adolescents. *Z. Kinderforsch.*, 35, 352-372.

PAINTER, G.B. (1964). The effect of rhythmic and sensory-motor activity programs on perceptual-motor-spatial abilities of kindergarten children. Unpublished M.S. dissertation, University of Illinois.

PASAMANICK, B., ROGERS, M.E. & LILLIENFELD, A.M. (1956). Pregnancy experience and development of behaviour disorder in children. *Am. J. Psychiat.*, 112, 613-618.

PASCALL, C.R. & SUTTELL, B.S. (1957). *The Bender-Gestalt Test.* New York: Grune & Stratton.

PETTIGREW, T. et al. (1967). *Racial Isolation in the Public Schools: a Report of the U.S. Commission on Civil Rights.* Washington, D.C.; United States Government Printing Office.

PIAGET, J. (1952). *The Origins of Intelligence in Children.* New York: International Universities Press.

PRECHTL, H.F.R. (1961). Neurological sequelae of pre-natal and paranatal complications. In B. Foss (Ed.) *Determinants of Infant Behaviour 1.* London: Methuen.

PRECHTL, H.F.R. (1963). The mother-child interaction in babies with minimal brain-damage. In B. Foss (Ed.) *Determinants of Infant Behaviour II.* London: Methuen.

PRECHTL, H.F.R. & STEMMER, C.J. (1962). The choreiform syndrome in children. *Dev. Med. Child. Neur.*, 8, 149-159.

RICHARDSON, S.A. (1964). The social environment and individual functioning. In H.G. Birch (Ed.) *Brain Damage in Children: the biological and social aspects.* Baltimore: Williams & Wilkins.

RITCHIE-RUSSELL, W. (1958). Disturbance of body image. *Cerebral Palsy Bull.*, 4, 7-9.

ROGERS, M., LILLIENFELD, A.M. &·PASAMANICK, B. (1955). Prenatal and paranatal factors in the development of childhood behaviour disorders. *Acta Psychiat. et Neur. Scand. Supplement* No. 101.

RUTTER, M., GRAHAM, P. & BIRCH, D. (1966). Intercorrelation between the choreiform syndrome, reading disability and psychiatric disorders. *Dev. Med. Child. Neur.* 8, 149-159.

SCHAFFER, H.R. (1965). Changes in developmental quotient under two conditions of maternal separation. *Brit. J. Soc. Clin. Psych.*, 4, 39-46.

SCHAFFER, H.R. (1966). Activity level as a constitutional determinant of infantile reaction to deprivation. *Child Dev.*, 37, 3, 592-602.

SCHAFFER, H.R. & EMERSON, P.E. (1968). The effects of experimentally administered stimulation on developmental quotients of infants. *Brit. J. Soc. Clin. Psych.*, 7, 61-67.

SCHILDER, P. (1935). *The Image and Appearance of the Human Body.* London: Kegan Paul.

SCHULZ, D.P. (1965). *Sensory Restriction.* New York: Academic Press.

SHERBORNE, V. (1965). Movement for mentally handicapped children. Bristol: Dept. of students of the National Assoc. of Mental Health.

SLOAN, W. (1948). *Lincoln Adaptation of the Oseretsky Scale.* Illinois: Lincoln.

SLOAN, W. (1955). The Lincoln/Oseretsky motor development scale. *Gen. Psych. Monog.*, 51, 183-252.

STEPHENSON, E. & ROBERTSON, J. (1965). Normal child development and handicapped children. In J.G. Howells (Ed.) *Modern Perspectives in Child Psychology.* Edinburgh: Oliver & Boyd.

STOTT, D.H. (1959). *Unsettled Children and Their Families.* London: Univ. Press.

STOTT, D.H. (1962). Evidence for a congenital factor in maladjustment and delinquency. *Am. J. Psych.*, 118, 781-794.

STOTT, D.H. (1964). Why maladjustment? *New Society*, Dec. 10th.

STOTT, D.H. (1966). A general test of motor-impairment for children. *Dev. Med. Child Neur.*, 8, 523-531.

STRAUSS, A.A. & LEHTINEN, L.C. (1948). *Psychopathology and Education of the Brain-injured Child.* New York: Grune & Stratton.

STRAUSS, A.A. & KEPHART, N.C. (1955). *Psychopathology and Education of the Brain-injured Child.* New York: Grune & Stratton.

SUTPHIN, F.E. (1964). *A Perceptual Testing-planning Handbook for First Grade Teachers.* New York: Boyd.

TANSLEY, A.E. & GULLIFORD, R. (1960). *The Education of Slow-learning Children.* London: Routledge & Kegan Paul.

TANSLEY, A.E. (1967). The education of neurologically abnormal children. *Times Educ. Suppl.*, Jan. 20th.

THWEATT, R.C. (1963). Prediction of school learning disabilities through the use of the Bender-Gestalt test. *J. Clin. Psych.*, 19, 216-217.

WALTON, J.H., ELLIS, E. & COURT, S.D.N. (1962). Clumsy children: developmental apraxia and agnosia. *Brain*, 85, 603.

WECHSLER, D. (1949). *Wechsler Intelligence Scale for Children–Manual.* New York: Psych. Corp.

WEDELL, K. (1964). *Some Aspects of Perceptual-motor Development in Young Children.* London: The Spastics Society.

WELFORD, A.T. (1968). *Fundamentals of Skill.* London: Methuen.

WERNER, H. (1941). Psychological approaches investigating differences in learning distractability. *Am. J. Ment. Def.*, 47, 269.

WHITING, H.T.A., JOHNSON, G.F. & PAGE, M. (1969). Factor analytic study of motor impairment at the ten-year age level in normal and E.S.N. populations. Unpublished paper, Physical Education Dept., University of Leeds.

WHITING, H.T.A. (1969). *Acquiring Ball Skill.* London: Bell.

WHITING, H.T.A., DAVIES, J.G., GIBSON, J.M., LUMLEY, R., SUT-CLIFFE, R.S.E. & MORRIS, P.R. (1970). Motor impairment in an approved school population. Unpublished paper, Physical Education Dept., University of Leeds.

WHITING, H.T.A. (1972a). Movement impairment. In J.D. Brooke & H.T.A. Whiting (Eds.) *Human Movement—a field of study.* London: Henry Kimpton.

WHITING, H.T.A. (1972b). Theoretical frameworks for an understanding of the acquisition of perceptual-motor skills. *Quest* **XVII**, 24-34.

WHITING, H.T.A., HARDMAN, K.H., HENDRY, L.B. & JONES, M.G. (1974). *Personality and Performance in Physical Education and Sport.* London: Henry Kimpton.

WITKIN, H.A., DYK, R.B., FATERSON, M.F. & KARP, S.A. (1962). *Psychological Differentiation.* New York: Wiley.

WITKIN, H.A. (1967). A cognitive style approach to cross-cultural research. *Int. J. Psych.,* **2, 4,** 232-250.

WRIGHT, B.A. (1960). *Physical Disability—a psychological approach.* New York: Harper & Row.

YARMOLENKO, A. (1933). The motor sphere of school-age children. *J. Genet. Psych.,* **42,** 298-316.

6

SOCIAL CONSTRAINTS ON SKILL LEARNING

6 SOCIAL CONSTRAINTS ON SKILL LEARNING

Some years ago, in the context of children with impaired psychomotor performance, we made the following statement:

> Each impaired child must be considered not as simply belonging to a homogeneous category but as an individual, his subnormal psycho-motor functioning must be viewed not as an isolated phenomenon but as part of his total situation—his condition is the result of a mutually inclusive amalgam of physiological, environmental and interpersonal factors (Morris and Whiting, 1971).

Having made this kind of statement, I think it is true to say that the major concern of workers in the field of skill acquisition has been with the mechanisms involved with very little attention being paid to the way in which such mediating mechanisms are built up through experience and how their development may be accelerated or retarded by the nature of that experience. Some of the possibilities in this respect were discussed in Section 4 under the significance of movement for development. If this contention is correct, it would be true to say that even less attention has been given to the broader category of interpersonal factors—what I shall call social constraints on skill learning—and the way in which they may retard performance.

Where attention has been given to such social implications, it has generally been the effects which retarded perceptual-motor skill development has on the social development of the young child. These in themselves are important considerations and I want to begin by developing some of these possibilities. At an everyday level, the problem is well appreciated by concerned parents and this was illustrated in Section 5 by the letters reproduced there and to which the reader is again referred.

There are two important considerations which need to be borne in mind:

1 The 'status significance' that competence in physical skills carries at

particular stages of childhood and the effect this might have on the development of the individual's self-esteem (Morris and Whiting, 1971; Hewett et al, 1970; Jones and Bayley, 1950).

In play, children often become accepted into social groupings on the basis of their competence to perform those physical skills which are characteristic of their age and neighbourhood—to ride a bike, to walk on stilts, to play hop-scotch, to skip etc. Any inability in these areas marks them out clearly as failures so that they become the subjects of adverse comment, are excluded from activities of this nature and often forced to play with children younger than themselves but representing their level of competence. Social exclusion might then be expected to have an effect on future psychomotor development.

> 2 The interaction between mother and infant which results in tension patterns in the mother (Barker and Wright, 1955; Richardson, 1964; Fairweather and Illsley, 1960; Casler, 1968; Prechtl, 1963; Stott, 1962; Hewett et al, 1970).

A child with impaired or low level motor skill performance may not only be a handicap to himself, but also to his mother. The way in which the mother views the handicap may have pronounced effects on the later psychomotor development of the child. She may feel guilty for example—that in some way the difficulty is her fault and could have been avoided. This may result in her becoming overprotective and in so doing depriving the child of the kind of experience necessary for physical skill development and an integrated body-concept. Even if this only takes the form of verbal conditioning against overdoing things or participating in any activity in which there may be an element of danger, the possible limitations on development are profound. Again, she may feel embarrased about her child's poor physical performances—at an extreme, to the extent that she deprives the child of social contact fearing the scorn that may fall on the child or herself for producing such a retarded child.

The deprivation to which reference is being made here, may not be restricted to those children who are impaired or of low perceptual-motor ability. Very often the 'good' child—in the sense that he does not demand attention—could be in a social deprivation situation. Because he is quiet, undemanding, relatively inactive, may lead to his receiving comparatively less attention from both the mother and other people in the environment. The way in which such lack of social interaction might operate is well illustrated in a series of studies by Schaffer and his co-workers.

In the first study to which reference is made Schaffer (1965) reports an interesting comparison between two groups of infants undergoing a temporary period (2-9 months) of institutionalisation. The staff-child ratio (an index of deprivation) in the 'hospitalised' group (the more deprived) was 1:6 and in the 'baby home' group (an institution for children who had been in contact with T.B. though they themselves were not ill) 1:2.5. The hospitalised infants received minimal environmental changes in that they remained in their cots for the majority of their stay while the baby home infants were taken from their dormitory to the gardens (where they spent some time) twice a day. The developmental quotients of the hospitalised infants during their stay were found to be significantly lower than those of the less-deprived infants. While no progressive deterioration of scores took place during the institutionalisation, the developmental quotients of the deprived group quickly matched those of the non-deprived group shortly after returning home. Schaffer interprets this temporary decrement in performance (and also in amount of vocalisation and activity) in terms of a depressant effect on 'arousal' due to insufficient stimulation. While maturation continues to take place (since no progressive deterioration occurs) the failure of the environment to arouse potentially available responses results in the infant functioning below his optimal level. The reader will be reminded of the learning/performance dichotomy raised in Section 2.

In a further study, Schaffer (1966) draws attention to constitutionally determined differences in activity level and their interactions with the environment in a deprivation situation. Taking infants on a continuum of 'active . . . inactive' (in terms of the amount of spontaneous behaviour displayed), he was able to show that inactive infants are more likely to be adversely affected than are active infants in such situations. He maintains that such activity will lead to frequent changes in position resulting in access to new environmental stimuli and that the proprioceptive feedback so obtained increases the responsiveness of cortical areas to afferent stimulation resulting in increased responsiveness to external sources of stimulation (a point speculated upon in Section 4).

A follow-up study (Schaffer and Emerson, 1968) examined the effects of experimentally administered stimulation on the developmental quotients of infants. Results indicated that changes in developmental assessment scores can be readily produced by manipulating the amount of stimulus input to which an infant is exposed prior to the testing. Such changes are again interpreted in terms of changes in 'arousal' level. As these workers point out, young infants have only limited ability to produce self-stimulation and hence are dependent on their current environment for the necessary means to maintain 'arousal'. They make the additional salient point that the ability of the infant to produce certain responses is dependent not only on their behavioural repertoire but the opportunity to make such potential behaviour manifest by the maintenance of an optimal 'arousal' level.

Early Milestones

Even at a very tender age, mothers are well aware of what their children should be capable and they build up an expectancy that certain 'norms' must be reached. An interesting study by Eley, Healey and Smidt (1972) based on six selected gross motor skills:

1 rolling over	2 sitting alone
3 pulling to stand	4 walking holding onto furniture
5 standing alone	6 walking alone

indicated that mothers regardless of socio-economic status or number of previous children are generally aware of the ages at which early milestones of gross motor development appear.

It seems reasonable to suppose that if these are not achieved at the appropriate time that the mother should be concerned. Additionally, she may well be aware of children in the neighbourhood who are precocious in terms of such milestones. It will be appreciated that there are definite advantages to being an early maturing child as these skills have an influence on perception of self and acceptance by others. Children in a highly competitive household might find themselves pressurised to achieve milestones for which they are inherently incapable. Holt (1969) perhaps reflects this idea. In searching for an answer to the question why do children fail, he writes:-

Why do they fail?
They fail because they are afraid, bored and confused.
They are afraid, above all else, of failing, of disappointing or displeasing the many anxious adults around them, whose limitless hopes and expectations for them hang over their heads like a cloud.

Holt continues to illustrate operationally what he has in mind:-

All Fall long, I wondered why Jack fell down so much playing soccer. He is an agile, well co-ordinated boy. His balance is good. People don't knock him over. Why was he on the ground so often? Suddenly, the other day I had the answer. I discovered it while trying to control the tension that builds up in me when I play the flute . . . when I am trying to play an exercise at high speed I am under tension . . . I am less confident that I can get through without a mistake and as I play . . . communication channels become clogged up, co-ordination breaks down, and I make mistakes I have been fearing to make . . .

Well the reason Jack falls down is that this relieves him, for a few seconds, of the great tension that he is under when he plays soccer.

Being small he is afraid of crashing into bigger boys but he is also afraid of showing his fear, and resolutely tries to play the game as he feels he should.

As might be expected, babies do not react to failure as older children do and this is because they have not yet been made to feel that failure is shame, disgrace or a crime and they are not concerned with protecting themselves against everything that is not easy and familiar. When and under what circumstances does such pressure begin to manifest itself?

Thus it would seem that reactions to success or failure have sociocultural connotations and as Cratty (1969) suggests, as an individual learns a skill he is concerned with not only task specifics but how the culture expects one of his age, sex and background to perform. The young performer in particular is continually sensitive to the extent to which his performance level either coincides or falls short of cultural expectation. Cratty proposes that a large portion of the apprehension experienced when one attempts to perform relatively hazardous movements may relate to the social consequences of failure. The correlate of failure in such circumstances being anxiety.

The induced anxiety over achievement has prompted Sutton-Smith and Roberts (1964) to propose what they term a conflict-enculturation hypothesis related to both social learning and personality adjustment. Briefly the hypothesis is as follows:

> Child training induces conflict—particularly anxiety over achievement. This leads to anxiety about representations of such conflicts as they appear on a lesser scale within a given culture. Curiosity leads him to participate in what are models of his conflict situation and to act out these models on a lesser scale thereby reducing the conflict to understandable proportions. In addition, he has the chance to succeed.

On this basis, they propose that games as such have the general cultural function of contributing to the learning and adjustment of persons who must maintain a high level of achievement maturation if the general cultural norms are to be sustained. One wonders what happens to the children whose level of competence prevents their participating in such miniature achievement models?

The Effect of 'Fear' on Skill Development

What seems to be clear from the kind of points being made above—and this has been well discussed in a recent thesis by my student Pritchard (1973)—is that many children fail to make the most of their abilities or to recognise their full potential because of certain unsolved fears which inhibit their learning and performance.

Even at higher levels of competence:

> ... a child who has athletic prowess and is considered by others as superior may suddenly face failure. This is a different reaction to the one given previously for rather than publicly face what to him must be the acceptance of inferiority, he will develop a reaction by which he will attempt to avoid situations where his superiority will be put to the test. This may result in a person who is stable but whose level of anxiety depends on his successfully avoiding situations which might upset his equilibrium. The danger here, is in deciding whether the individual is inhibited or lacking in abilities, for clumsiness in games is a disability which is rarely regarded as due to neurotic symptoms caused by inhibition and which could vanish when the cause of the inhibition is put right (Pritchard, 1973).

The deleterious effect of fear on perceptual-motor performance is so well recognised as not to need stating. While certain fears, such as fear of heights, enclosed or open spaces may well have innate origins, fear of ridicule, danger of harm, and threats may well have social origins. These suggestions may well be important in physical education which provides many potential fear-involving situations. Furthermore, while such situations may lead to the expressions or feeling of fear in the child, knowledge of the causes of such fearful behaviour in a given situation might result in the child being handled in a way that might overcome such fear. It seems reasonable to suggest that fear induction arising from environmental influences may be easier to understand and control than one which has innate origins.

In looking at the problems encountered by the persistent non-swimmer—particularly the head going under the water—we suggested some years ago (Whiting and Stembridge, 1965) that:

> ... presumably this fear of water is not an innate fear, since it does not appear to have been reported as such in the literature, and certainly the very young baby in the arms of a confident mother or nurse could appear to show pleasure rather than fear in contact with water.

It would seem therefore that fear of water is a learned phenomenon and this may well relate back to the child's early relationships with its parents—particularly the mother:

> It seems reasonably clear, that the persistent non-swimmer is not so because he lacks the potential for developing the physical skill of

swimming . . . The root cuase of the inability is almost entirely fear of the water or of the swimming situation itself (Whiting, 1970).

Attitudes (including fears)—as James (1950) suggests are communicated to the infant from the earliest moments and reflect his behaviour. It has further been proposed that such attitudes are mediated both by the personality of the child and that of the parent. In a study of personality and the persistent non-swimmer, (Whiting and Stembridge, 1965) we were able to show that persistent non-swimmers were more introverted and more neurotic (in Eysenck's terms) than were swimmers. This was interpreted in terms of the ease of conditioning to fear of the water characteristic of the introverted personality particularly with a labile autonomic nervous system (index of neuroticism). The way in which such fear of water may develop is illustrated in a recent study by Bentler (1962) which described how an infant's phobia to water developed as the result of a traumatic shock with a resultant conditioned fear. Bentler's subject—a year-old female child—acquired phobic reactions to water after slipping over in a bath-tub. Up to that time, water and bathing had been enjoyable experiences. After the traumatic event, the child would not go near water in any circumstances and some form of therapy in this extreme case was a necessity for normal development.

The reaction of Bentler's subject was an example of single-trial conditioning occurring in early childhood. It is not clear to what extent the parent of the child was instrumental in this case but such a possibility seems highly likely. Previously we noted that similar instances of fear may be involved by verbal conditioning, often by anxious and over-protective parents who may themselves have had similar responses to water situations. That the personality of the parent may affect the development of the child, is implicit in the following statement by Mussen et al (1969):

> If the mother herself is afraid of an object or event, she cannot do anything to make it less fear-provoking for her child. Consequently he continues to fear the stimulus and to make avoidance and withdrawal responses. For these reasons fears which the child shares with his mother are particularly resistant to treatment and extinction.

In an unpublished study by Jennings and Livingstone (1970) into personality and the persistent non-swimmer, the ability of the parents to swim was also recorded. While there were no significant differences in the number of fathers who could swim in the two categories of swimmer and persistent non-swimmer, the picture was different for the mothers. A highly significant difference in the number of mothers who could not swim with children who were persistent non-swimmers as compared with mothers who could not swim and whose children could swim was reported. This finding was also reinforced by the number of mothers who accompanied their persistent non-swimming children to the remedial sessions—even at secondary level!

References

BARKER, R.G. & WRIGHT, H.F. (1955). *Midwest and Its Children: the psychological ecology of an American Town.* New York: Row & Peterson.

BENTLER, P.M. (1962). An infant's phobia treated with reapproval inhibition therapy. *J. Child Psych. Psychiat.,* 3.

CASLER, L. (1968). Perceptual deprivation in institutional settings. In A. Newton & S. Levine (Eds.) *Early Experience and Behaviour.* Springfield: Thomas.

CRATTY, B.J. (1969). *Perceptual Motor Behaviour and Educational Processes.* Springfield: Thomas.

ELEY, K.P., HEALEY, A. & SMIDT, G.L. (1972). Mother's expectations of their child's accomplishments of certain gross motor skills. *Dev. Med. Child. Neur.,* 14, 621-625.

FAIRWEATHER, O.V. & ILLSLEY, R. (1960). Obstetric and social origins of mentally handicapped children. *Brit. J. Prev. Soc. Med.,* 14, 149-159.

HEWETT, S., NEWSON, J. & NEWSON, E. (1970). *The Family and the Handicapped Child.* London: Allen & Unwin.

HOLT, J. (1969). *How Children Fail.* Harmondsworth: Penguin.

JAMES, W. (1950). *The Principles of Psychology.* London: Dover.

JENNINGS, P.L. & LIVINGSTONE, J. (1970). An investigation of the psychological factors affecting the persistent non-swimmer and a comparison of two teaching methods. Unpublished Diploma of Physical Education Dissertation: University of Leeds.

JONES, M.C. & BAYLEY, N. (1950). Physical maturing among boys as related to behaviour. *J. Educ. Psych.,* 41, 129-148.

MORRIS, P.R. & WHITING, H.T.A. (1971). *Motor Impairment and Compensatory Education.* London: Bell.

MUSSEN, P.H. et al (1969). *Child Development and Personality.* London: Harper & Row.

PRECHTL, H.F.R. (1963). The mother-child interaction in babies with minimal brain-damage. In B. Foss (Ed.) *Determinants of Infant Behaviour II.* London: Methuen.

PRITCHARD, O.H. (1973). Fear and performance. Unpublished M.A. dissertation. Department of Physical Education: University of Leeds.

RICHARDSON, S.A. (1964). The social environment and individual functioning. In H.G. Birch. (Ed.) *Brain Damage in Children: the biological and social aspects.* Baltimore: Williams and Wilkins.

SCHAFFER, H.R. (1965). Changes in developmental quotient under two conditions of maternal separation. *Brit. J. Soc. Clin. Psych.*, **4**, 39-46.

SCHAFFER, H.R. (1966). Activity level as a constitutional determinant of infantile reaction to deprivation. *Child Dev.*, **37**, 592-602.

SCHAFFER, H.R. & EMERSON, P.E. (1968). The effects of experimentally administered stimulation on developmental quotients of infants. *Brit. J. Soc. Clin. Psych.*, **7**, 61-67.

STOTT, D.H. (1962). Evidence for a congenital factor in maladjustment and delinquency. *Am. J. Psych.*, **118**, 781-794.

SUTTON-SMITH, B. & ROBERTS, J.M. (1964). Rubrics of competitive behaviour *J. Genet. Psychol.*, **105**, 13-37.

WHITING, H.T.A. & STEMBRIDGE, D.E. (1965). Personality and the persistent non-swimmer. *Res. Quart.*, 36.

WHITING, H.T.A. (1970). *Teaching the Persistent Non-swimmer*. London: Bell.

7

INFORMATION PROCESSING IN BALL SKILLS – AN EXPERIMENTAL APPROACH

7 INFORMATION PROCESSING IN BALL SKILLS – AN EXPERIMENTAL APPROACH

This section consists of two parts. In Part 1 a series of experiments developed logically from one another and giving rise to practical illustration of some of the concepts raised in previous sections is presented. Part 2 reports a further series of experiments devised and carried out by my research student Robert Sharp* which questions some of the earlier interpretations and in so doing, extends our knowledge and understanding of psychological factors involved in ball-skill acquisition.

Part 1

The motivation for carrying out the experimental work on which Part 1 of this section is based, arises from a questioning of the validity of some of the principles which coaches and teachers take for granted.

Some of the statements, the validity of which is in question, follow:

(i) The question of whether the left arm is straight in the golf swing or whether a fast hand action is necessary in the impact zone. Recent photographic techniques had answered 'no' to the first question and 'yes' to the second. Only when comparative and more sophisticated camera techniques were used late in 1967 was the fallacy of these 'accepted' interpretations brought into question (Whiting, 1969).

(ii) Look at the ball and not the hole when putting in golf! Evidence in support of this contention does not appear to have been provided although it would appear to be accepted as axiomatic within the game. Probe experiments carried out by my own students suggest that such evidence may not be forthcoming or at least will need to

---

*Now at Jordanhill College of Physical Education, Glasgow, Scotland.

123

be qualified by reference to the standard of the player and the way in which he has received his initial training.

(iii) Keep the eye on the ball! This is a standardised instruction in practically all text books. Where not quoted, it is generally taken as axiomatic. Little is ever said about the conditions under which this statement is valid in terms of experience of the player, type of situation etc., and yet we know for example that purely from the limitations imposed by a person's reaction time, that it is pointless—from an information viewpoint—to keep the eye on the ball *all* the time. There may be other reasons for doing so—such as mechanical efficiency—but this is seldom if ever made explicit.

If we stay with this latter question of *keeping the eye on the ball*, since this is the area upon which much of my experimental work has concentrated, the theoretical position has been put fairly explicitly by Kay (1957):

We may compare this situation with the case of someone trying to estimate the future position of a moving object say a car or the trajectory of a ball from a limited observation of its initial stages. If we throw a ball for a young child to catch he is invariably too late in positioning his hands and lets the ball hit him on the chest. We say he doesn't anticipate the flight of the ball; he doesn't know where it will go but only where it is. Let us imagine the situation is such that our adult subject's head is fixed and he can only observe the trajectory of the ball by successive fixations. Thus we have the trajectory divided into a series of segments which one might think of as events a, b, c and so on. An individual through his experience of watching how objects travel in space learns about the probable order and temporal relations of these events. Thus, given events a, b, c he predicts the future position: and the skilled person is the one who can predict accurately on the fewest possible initial events. Once this is achieved the remaining events in the series are redundant or at the most confirmatory. So much for the popular dictum about 'keeping your eye on the ball'.

Thus, Kay's (1957) theoretical exposition suggests that the experienced player at least does not need to keep his eye on the ball all the time, since he learns the sequential dependencies of information about the various parts of the ball trajectory and is thus able to anticipate its future position. It should be noted in this respect that there is a difference between being able to anticipate *spatially* the future position of a ball in flight and being able to *temporally* organise a response in relation to such information. These two considerations will be taken up later in the article. They have been well illustrated in a recent paper by Alderson, Sully and Sully (1974).

From an experimental design point of view, two procedures seemed to be appropriate for testing Kay's theoretical position:

1 A field study in which the actual behaviour of games players was observed in the playing situation and differences between particular criterion groups of players recorded and analysed.

2 A laboratory contrived situation in which opportunities for viewing the ball in flight were restricted and observations made on the effect that this has on learning and performance.

Although the first kind of approach seemed to offer the most promise of applied development, it was not feasible to proceed in this direction because of the financial limitations involved in for example the purchase of such equipment as an eye-movement camera. All experimental work carried out to date has therefore been laboratory contrived.

In the initial probe experiments (Whiting, 1967) I was able to show that in a laboratory task which involved the continuous aiming and catching of a ball kept captive on the end of a chain (Fig. 10) subjects were able to maintain their performance standards under restricted lighting conditions after a period of practice in full-light. The results of these probe experiments suggested that it might be worth looking at the effect of training people on a similar task under restricted light conditions with a view to short-circuiting the training procedures. That is to say, if reasonably expert performers were able to keep up a high standard when performing under limited viewing conditions, it seemed possible that subjects trained from the beginning under such conditions might achieve optimal performance in a quicker time. The possible misinterpretation in this respect has been suggested by Whiting (1969) since it seems apparent that beginners at a particular skill do not utilise the same kind of information as the expert does. To extrapolate therefore from what the expert does to what we think the beginner *ought* to do can be very misleading. Although some subjects were able to achieve standards of performance under restricted-light viewing conditions equivalent to those trained in full-light, the interpretation was not quite so straightforward. (Fig.11). One of the complications in this experiment was that when the subjects were tested in full-light after their training under restricted light conditions, it seemed possible that they simply reverted to the method of performance they had adopted on the first test trial under full-light i.e. their training programme had not been transferred. This idea raised the problem of teaching for transfer which was not unfortunately controlled in this experiment.

Bearing in mind the artificiality of the situation in this experiment (since subjects were forced to view the ball at *particular* times), it was decided to adopt a more flexible approach with similar apparatus such that subjects

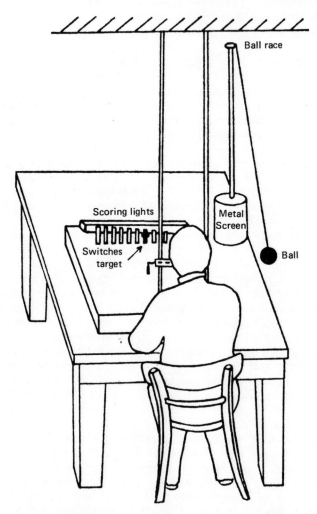

Fig. 10. Modified table-skittle apparatus (Whiting, 1969).

could have the ball lit-up (in an otherwise dark room) or the target but not both together (Whiting, 1970). Over a period of training sessions, subjects were then left free to adjust their viewing time of ball or target in a manner which they found most suitable in an effort to obtain the highest possible scores (a combination of *speed* and *accuracy*). Overall results of this experiment indicated a decrease in the amount of time the ball was watched

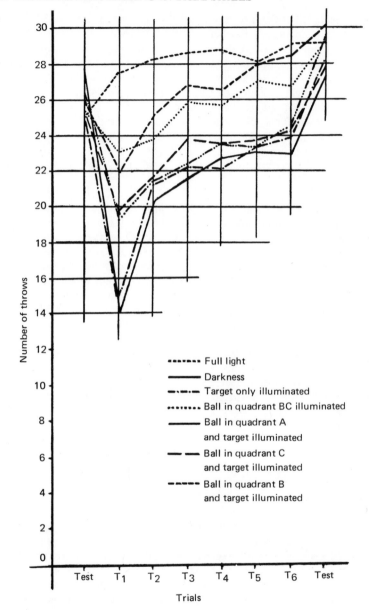

Fig. 11. Results of training players under full-light and restricted light conditions (Whiting, 1969).

while it was in flight from session to session. This result was paralleled by an increase in the amount of time before the ball reached the hand that the eyes transferred from the ball to the target. Thus, once again some support was given to the theoretical position that as subjects become more proficient they need to watch the ball less and less up to some optimum level for the individual. It should be noted that in all the experiments carried out to date marked individual differences were apparent.

If Kay's theoretical position is correct, and the limits of the last experiment are borne in mind, the next question which posed itself was:

> . . . are there critical time intervals for taking in flight information in a ball-catching task?

In all the previous experiments, *outflow* information was available to the subject since he initiated the ball-flight (whether in fact such information was used is another question) and it was not clear to what extent information from the environment was in itself of importance and whether or not speed of processing such information was a critical factor. This led to the design of a piece of apparatus for the next experiment (Whiting et al, 1970) which simulated an actual catching situation. That is to say, that the ball (which could be illuminated internally) was dropped on to a ramp and caused to enter on to a roughly parabolic flight path such as might occur in a number of game situations (Fig. 12). The experiment was carried out once again in a photographic dark-room and the ball—after hitting the ramp (trampette)—was caused to light up for periods of time ranging from 0.1 to 0.4 secs. The subject standing at a distance of ten feet away was required to catch the ball with one hand. Scoring was based on the number of successful catches made out of twenty on each of the restricted light conditions.

Overall results indicated that the longer the subject was able to view the ball in flight, the better was his catching performance (Fig. 13). However some subjects were able to produce results at the 0.1 and 0.15 sec. treatment levels which were remarkably good. Nine subjects had catches of nine or more at 0.1 secs. and eighteen achieved this level of success at 0.15 secs. Once again the overall results masked considerable individual differences.

The results of this batch of experiments raise several pertinent questions. For example, how quickly can information concerned with characteristics of ball flight be processed? Can the experienced performer process this information faster than the inexperienced performer or is the reason for the difference in the speed of responding due primarily to the shorter reaction times of the former (since as Poulton, 1965 has suggested, it is unlikely that anyone with slow reactions will excel in fast ball games, but at the same time points out that to excel will require more than fast reactions)?

With these questions in mind, an experiment was designed to examine the

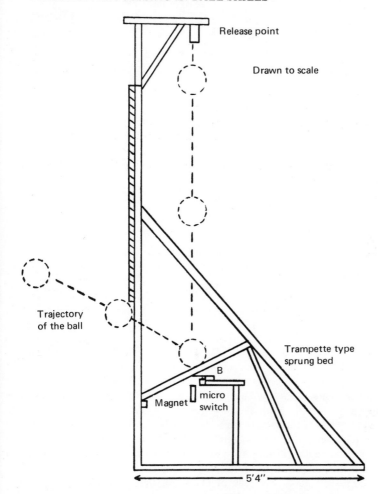

Fig. 12. Ball-dropping gantry (Whiting, Gill & Stephenson, 1970).

effects of *personality* and *ability* on speed of decisions regarding the directional aspects of ball flight (Whiting and Hutt, 1972). A choice reaction time task (C.R.T.) and a task which involved judging the directional aspects of ball flight (B.F.T.) were administered to three groups of subjects defined as high ability table-tennis players (N=13), average ability table-tennis players (N=18) and non-games players (N=15).

Apparatus for the C.R.T. task comprised three yellow neon bulbs mounted

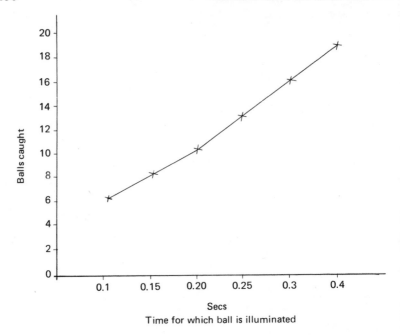

Fig. 13. Number of balls caught (out of 20) under differing periods of illumination (Whiting, Gill & Stephenson, 1970).

on a black background serving as the stimulus panel and the subjects' response keys were the same as in the B.F.T. task. For the latter task, subjects were required to observe table-tennis balls projected on to a table-tennis table by a **STIGA** automatic table-tennis machine. The impact point for the ball (Fig.14) was directly in the centre of an aperture 3″ x 3¾″ of a black screen which hid the equipment from the subject's view. Photoelectric cells attached to the Experimenter's (E's) side of the screen were positioned so that each ball passed through the light beam immediately prior to hitting the table thereby activating a millisecond timer. Covering the aperture was a fringe made up of strips of fine black tissue paper which, while allowing the table-tennis ball to pass unimpeded, eradicated the possibility of the subject viewing the balls on their downward flight path from the machine. By altering the projection angle of the wheels of the **STIGA** robot, balls could be projected with or without sidespin so that on striking the table they would travel either directly towards the subject or deviate to his right or left by ten degrees.

The subject was seated at a small raised table, 15 feet from the screen. In order to mask extraneous sound, headphones were worn through which white

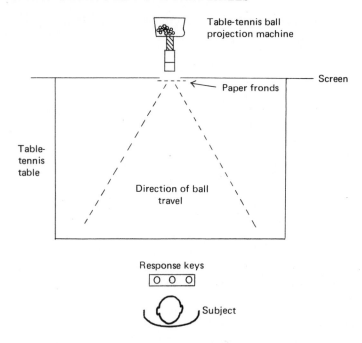

Fig. 14. Table-tennis machine apparatus (Whiting & Hutt, 1972).

noise was fed. A chin rest was provided to standardise the head position. In front of the subject were three response keys for the subject to indicate whether the ball was to the right, left or straight towards him, the depression of which stopped the timer and activated an appropriate light on E's side of the screen to indicate whether the response was correct.

A personality inventory (Eysenck and Eysenck, 1964) was administered to all subjects.

An analysis of the B.F.T. task in terms of personality (extraversion and neuroticism) failed to show any significant differences. However, significant differences were found between the *ability* groups in both the C.R.T. and B.F.T. tasks. The relationship between subjects' times for the two tasks were found to be significant for the non-games players and average ability table-tennis players but not for the high ability table-tennis players.

Thus, results of this investigation failed to support previous findings cited by Eysenck (1967) which showed that extraverts were more predisposed to speed at the risk of making a greater number of errors than introverts. However several previous investigators' findings were based on the results of neurotic subjects e.g. Brierly (1961) and Foulds (1951). Even with such subjects, Himmelweit (1946) could only find an inverse relationship between speed and accuracy on a manipulative type task. More recently Gibson (1969) and Hendry (1970) have demonstrated such a relationship between personality characteristics and a preference for speed or accuracy in performing on the Spiral Maze test, but little evidence is available in predominately perceptual tasks. One exception is the study by Shanmugan (1965) who reported a reaction time task in which subjects were asked to discriminate between two lines in which the differences in length varied. The easier discriminations produced no significant differences between introverts and extraverts, but when discriminations were more difficult, extraverts were shown to be significantly faster than introverts. Perhaps the present study could be likened to Shanmugan's easier discrimination task. Considering the speed and angles of the projected balls and that subjects had only to discriminate differences in direction, only a minimal amount of information needed to be sampled before a decision was made with a high degree of confidence. If the present task had been designed so that discriminations were more difficult, such effects due to personality differences may have been evidenced although—as Brim et al (1962) point out—variability due to personality characteristics in decision-making tasks may be outweighed by other factors; in this investigation by situational and ability variables.

Further evidence has therefore been produced to support Poulton's (1965) contention that generally a person with a slow reaction time is unlikely to achieve a reasonable level of proficiency in fast ball games. The results of this experiment have shown in addition that such a factor is unable to differentiate the player of high ability from the player of average ability. This is not surprising; the level of performance exhibited by a subject in a choice reaction time task in a laboratory situation may only have a slight relationship with his speed of decision making in a game, since any limitations that may be imposed by a comparatively slow reaction time may be considerably reduced by the experienced player through the correct identification of perceptual cues which will lead to a decrease in the uncertainty of the display and an enhancement of anticipatory behaviour.

A comparison of decision time and choice reaction time indicates that speed in detecting the direction of movement (as measured in this experiment) was highly dependent upon the subject's choice reaction time for the *average ability* and *non games group*, but was markedly less for the *high ability group*. This latter result could be partially accounted for in terms of greater familiarity with the swerving table tennis ball flight usually encountered only at higher levels of table-tennis, or the utilisation of different information, since one subject remarked that the future direction of flight could be detected from the direction of spin on the ball as it hit the table-tennis table. A more likely explanation is provided by the highly significant negative correlation between the decision times and errors of the high ability group which suggests that subjects adopted different strategies in the ball flight task.

It is interesting to speculate that this greater disposition of the high ability group to trade speed for accuracy or accuracy for speed may be reflective of a defensive or attacking set which seems to be characteristic of certain players in the game.

Part 2

While the experiments described in Part 1 have provided some clarification of the way in which information is sampled during ball skill acquisition and performance, there are a number of problems which have not been solved and moreover, some of the interpretations of these early experimental results need to be questioned.

It will be recalled that the interpretation of the decreased catching performance in these experiments was based on limitations in the amount of time for which the ball could be viewed prior to hand contact. However, performance strictly speaking could not necessarily be accounted for by the length of the *viewing period* because of an uncontrolled co-varying factor. That factor was the interval between the end of the viewing period and the moment of ball capture. Thus, it was not possible to conclude whether increasing the viewing period, decreasing the subsequent occluded period (time for which ball was in darkness) or their combined effect was responsible for variations in performance.

The paradigm for the factors now raised is illustrated in Fig. 15. DP represents the *variable* period for which the room is in darkness from the moment of projection to the moment at which the room is first illuminated. VP represents the time interval for which the room and hence the ball is actually illuminated. OP and LP represent the remainder of time for which the ball is occluded in flight. The distinction between OP and LP is a conceptual one necessitated by the fact that the period of occlusion following VP cannot have an effect right up to the moment of ball-hand contact. There is in fact an interval preceding this moment which is equivalent to a CNS latency *plus* movement time, during which any change in the stimulus conditions will have no effect on the subject's response. For the purposes of these experiments, this interval is considered constant and hence the *effective* occluded period—the variable of interest—is the interval between light offset and the LP (i.e. the period OP).

Pilot work showed that LP was approximately 200 msecs. and that total flight time i.e. the period from ball projection to ball-hand contact, was approximately 580 msecs.

In the first of these experiments (Whiting and Sharp, 1974) VP was held

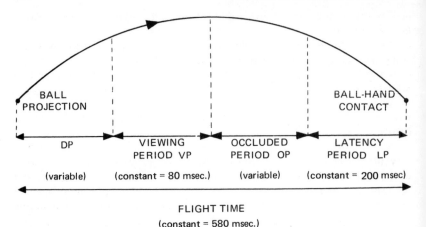

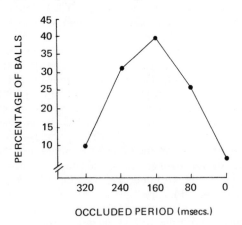

Fig. 15. Viewing conditions paradigm (Whiting & Sharp, 1974).

constant at 80 msecs. so that by varying DP, OP was free to vary between 0
and 375 msecs. OP in fact was varied between 0 and 320 msecs in five equal
steps of 80 msecs.

Subjects were required to catch tennis balls delivered by a mechanical
projection machine (loaded-spring type). They performed under all the OP
conditions suitably counterbalanced to take account of any residual effects of
one particular occluded period following another.

*Fig. 16. Percentage of balls caught under different occluded periods (Whiting & Sharp,
1974).*

The results for the percentage of balls caught at the different occluded periods is illustrated in Fig. 16. Statistical analysis showed OP to be a reliable source of variation in performance. Moreover, all adjacent pairwise OP comparisons were shown to be significantly different thus supporting the contention that success in a ball-catching task would be significantly influenced by the occluded period following sight of the ball. Thus, the relation between viewing period and catching success reported in the earlier experiments may have been due in part to the subsequent period of occlusion covarying with the viewing period.

An interpretation of these findings throws some light on the statement by Kay (1957) (page 124) previously quoted when it was suggested that in catching a ball a two-stage process is possibly involved:

1   A spatial prediction problem in terms of where the ball will be when caught.
2   A temporal prediction problem in terms of when will it get there and how can an interception movement be carried out.

The decline in performance between OP = 160 msecs and 320 msecs. suggests that the subject experiences increasing difficulties because he has to predict ball flight over successively longer intervals of time. This may be due to the increasing decay of information in immediate memory or to the subject having to construct or represent the flight path over longer distances. The latter interpretation seems more tenable.

The most interesting feature of the present results is the curvilinear relationship between catching performance and OP. If the OP effect was due *solely* to prediction limitations, then performance would be expected to increase as the OP was reduced from 160 msecs. to 0 msecs. As the trend was in fact the reverse, an answer must be sought elsewhere. One explanation is that when sight of the ball is not allowed until very late, the subject does not have sufficient time to process the necessary flight information. Also, he may not have time to translate this perception of the ball's flight into an appropriate response pattern. Both of these processes imply information-processing limitations.

In this experiment, the question still remains as to whether the observed OP effects were an artefact of the particular VP employed (held constant at 80 msecs). Varying VP in the earlier studies was shown to affect performance even though this effect was confounded with OP. It is possible that catching performance in these experiments is dependent upon the *joint* effects of VP and OP.

An attempt was made to investigate this question and thus clarify the effect of OP (Sharp and Whiting, 1974). A similar catching task was given to the subject but this time with manipulation of both independent variables VP

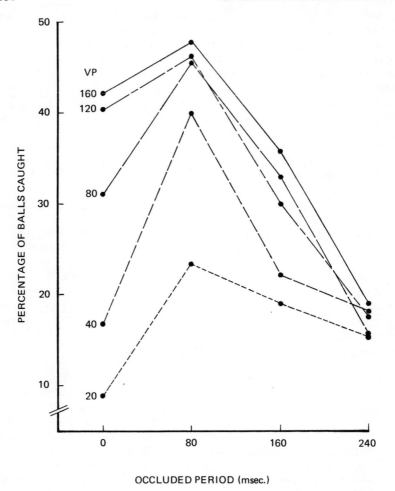

Fig. 17. Percentage of balls caught under the various OP/VP combinations. (Sharp & Whiting, 1974).

and OP. In addition, instead of subjects performing under all the OP conditions as in the last experiment, different groups of subjects performed under each of the OP conditions to ensure that the effect previously reported was not just a 'range' effect due to the order in which each of the different OP's were experienced. The OP was one of the levels 0, 80, 160, or 240 msecs. and the VP 20, 40, 80, 120 or 160 msecs. The results representing percentage catching performance under the various OP/VP combinations are shown in Fig. 17.

It will be noted that the curve for VP = 80 msec. is similar to that obtained in the previous experiment when subjects performed on all possible OP levels. Statistical analysis confirmed—what is apparent—that the OP effect is not simply a range effect.

The slightly better performance exhibited at all levels of OP in the current study can be considered due to sampling variability and/or a lower ball velocity making the task a little easier than before.

Overall, the results illustrate the dependence of ball-catching success on the *interactive* effects of VP and OP. Generally, the effect of VP is most clearly marked at the shorter occlusion periods and assumes less importance as OP is extended.

When OP is zero, increments in VP are followed by significant improvements in catching success until VP = 120 msecs. Presumably increasing VP within this range provides the subject with more time to see the ball and hence more time both to acquire relevant flight information and to translate his perception of such information into an appropriate spatio-temporal catching response. Unfortunately, it is not possible to differentiate these processes at present but it is worth noting that increases in VP as little as 20 msecs. can facilitate the entire process. At this stage, it would appear that the subject is limited by the amount of time he has to process flight information. This can be circumvented by increasing VP and also by increasing OP. Fig. 17 indicates that increasing OP by 80 msecs. leads to proportionate increases in performance for every level of VP.

An unexpected feature of these results is the apparent ceiling effect which is reflected in the non-significant difference between VP = 120 msecs. and 160 msecs. at OP = 0 msecs. and between VP = 40, 80, 120 and 160 msecs. at OP = 80 msecs. While this may represent a real ceiling effect caused by a general suppression in performance due to the unusual lighting conditions operating, it might well be that there is a non-linear relation between catching success and VP such that the effect of VP is less for greater durations than for smaller ones. This latter suggestion is hardly viable because the interaction between VP and OP suggests that catching performance should really be explained in terms of both these variables. It is considered that a more meaningful explanation would involve the *total time* available for processing i.e. VP + OP.

This interpretation is illustrated in Fig. 18 for all levels of VP at OP = 0 and 80 msecs. It can be seen that there is a systematic, negatively accelerating relationship between catching performance and the total time available for processing flight information. This relationship was quantified by a curve-fitting analysis which showed a parabolic function to account for 93% of the performance variance. Furthermore, this curve predicted almost 100% success when the ball could be seen for its entire flight.

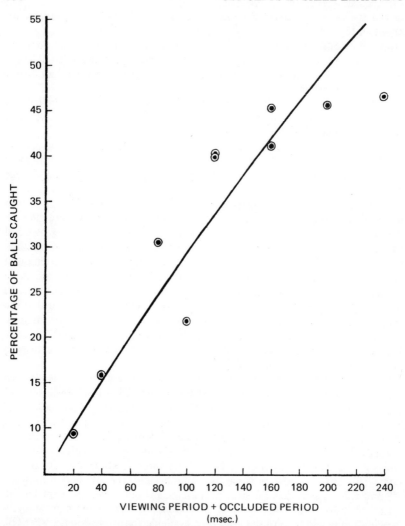

Fig. 18. Percentage of balls caught plotted against (VP + OP) (Sharp & Whiting, 1974).

It appears then that it is not the time the ball is seen *per se* which is important when processing flight information (although there will be a lower threshold duration) but the total time available (VP + OP). The evidence further suggests that it does not matter how VP and OP each contribute to the total time. Thus, the condition OP = 80 msecs. VP = 40 msecs. and OP =

0 msecs. VP = 120 msecs. both result in similar performance percentages as do the conditions OP = 80 msecs. VP = 80 msecs. and OP = 0 msecs. VP = 160 msecs.

This systematic relationship breaks down for occluded periods greater than 80 msecs. when performance decreases. It would seem that the additional processing time gained by incrementing OP beyond 80 msecs. is outweighted by other factors which are detrimental to performance. The simplest explanation is that those factors are concerned with motion prediction error. It is well known that motion prediction errors increase with prediction *extent* so that while increasing OP may provide additional processing time, it also increases prediction extent which, as it becomes larger, outweighs the advantage gained by the concomitant increase in processing time. The general curvilinear trend (Fig. 17) may represent the relative extent to which the two factors, information processing time and prediction extent each affect performance as OP is varied.

It is important to note that the interaction between VP and OP is still evident during the 'prediction' phase, i.e., when OP is greater than 80 msecs. Studies of motion prediction have often shown prediction extent to be the prime parameter governing performance and the time given for viewing the moving target to be of negligible importance. This effect is also evident in the current data when OP is maximal at 240 msecs., although not so when OP = 160 msecs. At this later level it is beneficial for S to have observed the ball for a longer period prior to the period of occlusion. This finding supports the hypothesis alluded to previously (page 137). It was suggested that S's inability to predict over longer intervals was due to his increasing uncertainty about the ball's flight path. From an information theory standpoint this hypothesis predicts that if S's uncertainty is reduced he will make fewer errors. If it is assumed that increasing VP provides S with more time to acquire flight information—an assumption implied previously—which in turn provides him with a more informative representation of the ball's trajectory then prediction over the occluded period should be easier for longer viewing periods. As this was found at OP = 160 msecs. then the thesis is supported. Presumably the reason why VP had no effect when OP is maximal is because the uncertainty associated with predicting over such a long interval is not reduced significantly by the information value of the greater VP. Perhaps extending VP further than 160 msecs. would have helped.

It will not have escaped the reader's attention that in the previous two experiments analysed, performance overall is relatively low—even under the best combination of lighting conditions, seldom exceeding 40 balls caught. The next problem then is to determine whether or not the observed relationship between 'total time' and catching success was continuously negatively accelerated as predicted by the previous curve fitting analysis, or whether this relationship represented a ceiling effect around 50% catching success possibly caused by the unfamiliar lighting conditions. It is also possible that the relationship is a step function with only the first portion being previously observed—in which case, catching performance could not be explained solely in terms of the variable total time.

A similar procedure to that used in the last two experiments was adopted. VP and OP were once again the two independent variables and the values of VP + OP (total time) were selected to cover the range used in the last experiment (Fig. 17) and also to extend first sight of the ball much closer to its projection point. Groups of subjects were randomly assigned to each of the seven selected total times 80, 120, 160, 140, 400 and 480 msecs. The various conditions to which subjects were assigned are given in Table 1.

		40	80	120	160	200	240	280	320	360	400	440	480
OCCLUDED PERIOD	0	S_1	S_1	S_2	S_3		S_4		S_5		S_6		S_7
	40	S_1	S_2	S_3		S_4		S_5		S_6		S_7	
	80	S_2	S_3		S_4		S_5		S_6		S_7		
	120	S_3			S_4		S_5		S_6		S_7		

Table 1 Table illustrating assignment of Ss to conditions (Each subscript indicates a different group of Ss).

Group 1 also operated under the total time 40 msecs. by receiving the condition VP = 40 msecs. OP = 0 msecs. Both groups 1 and 2 received additional conditions not given in the table viz. VP = 60 msecs. OP = 20 msecs. and VP = 60 msecs. OP = 60 msecs. respectively, thus making the total number of conditions within each group equal to four. The viewing conditions and the results which it is intended to discuss (those which were significant in the analysis) are shown in Fig. 19. The mean performance (percentage) under each total time is given in the right-hand column. The significant ($P < .05$ and $P < .01$) and non-significant (N.S.) comparisons between the groups are also shown. These results confirm that catching performance can be related to the parameter VP + OP up to about 120 msecs. This holds provided VP is above a threshold value in the region of 40 msecs. and OP is not greater than 80 msecs. The relationship between catching performance and total time breaks down between 120 and 240 msec. which would be expected only if this plateau represented a real ceiling effect in terms of catching success. As it does not, then an explanation other than that performance depends solely on total processing time must be sought for the equivalence of conditions having the same total time.

A possible explanation is that S uses only the portion of flight illuminated

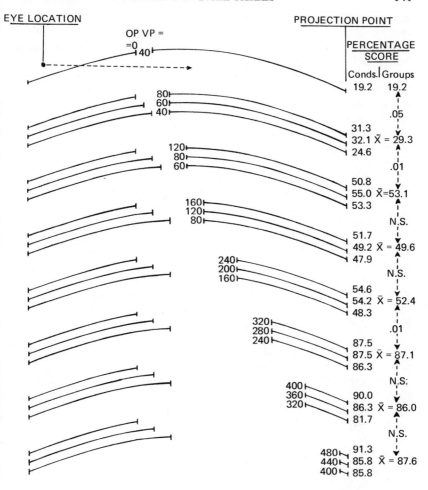

Fig. 19. Viewing conditions and catching performance under selected VP/OP conditions.

first. This could arise in two ways. Firstly, the nature of the experimental design was such that the ball always came into view at the same time (for any particular *S*). Additionally, knowledge of how long the ball is visible was unavailable. On this basis *S*s may have adopted some kind of expectancy behaviour in which their attentional capacity was directed only to the portion of flight that was certain of being seen—the initial portion. This solution does not specifically account for the plateau between 120 and 240 msec. however, and for this reason a second explanation is favoured.

According to subjective evidence it was found easy to maintain fixation before ball projection, but this may not continue when the ball is in flight. The normal eye movement response to a moving target involves an initial reaction time latency and then a saccade to meet the target. At this moment the eyes begin following the moving target (providing its angular velocity is not too high), thus maintaining a stable retinal image. From this it can be seen that depending on the length of time the ball is viewed, information about its motion may be provided by either one, or both of two different motion detecting systems—the image/retina and eye/head movement systems. If the viewing period is too short, ball motion will be picked up only as the retinal image 'paints' the retinae, and hence via the image/retina system. If long enough for pursuit tracking however, then additional information is provided by the eye/head system. Now because Ss operate under conditions in which the ball always first appears at the same time it would be expected that when they had learned this invariance (Ss indicated this did occur) they could reduce the saccadic latency to meet the ball. It is possible therefore that S can begin his saccade very shortly after light onset, and for each condition with the same total time at approximately the same moment in time. Thus, on those occasions when the total time does not permit pursuit tracking, performance is constant for every condition with the same total time because Ss' eye movements effectively makes them the same.

The relationship between total time and catching performance can be explained in the same context. The initial increase up to 120 msec. may be seen to represent the effect of increasing the time to process information provided by the image/retina system. The plateau between 120 and 240 msec. may be connected with the 'quality' of this information. In this respect, if S begins a saccade so shortly after light onset that the image provided by the image/retina system is very poor, e.g., it may approach threshold, then performance would not be expected to increase when the total time, and hence processing time, was increased beyond a certain duration. The plateau may thus be seen to represent a ceiling effect in terms of the amount of information processed. The sharp rise after this plateau may reflect the assimilation of additional motion information through the eye/head system, this being possible due to the increased length of the viewing period. The final plateau probably represents a true ceiling effect, it being submaximal only through incidental factors such as fatigue, and attentional lapses etc.

The above explanation is consistent with the data except for one apparent anomaly. It was suggested that pursuit tracking was possible when the total time is 320 msec. or greater but not when less than or equal to 240 msec. Why therefore, should pursuit be possible in the condition VP = 240, OP = 80 msec. but not in the condition VP = 240, OP = 0 msec. when the actual viewing period is the same in both? It happens that in the former condition first sight of the ball is closer to S's initial direction of fixation than in the latter condition. This means that saccadic movement will be less, which in turn results in both a shorter latency and a shorter movement time. S thus has additional time available in the former condition which may be sufficient to initiate smooth pursuit and hence result in superior performance.

This investigation has raised many questions but in doing so has highlighted a factor which may be of fundamental importance in the field situation. That factor is the nature of the performer's eye movement behaviour which is, in turn, inextricably linked to the visual perception of object motion.

For an extension of the ideas presented in Part 2, the reader is referred to Sharp (1975).

References

ALDERSON, G.J.K., SULLY, D.J. & SULLY, H.G. (1974). An operational analysis of a one-handed catching task using high speed photography. *J. Motor Beh.*, **6**, 217-226.

BRIERLEY, H., (1961). The speed and accuracy characteristics of neurotics. *Brit. J. Psychol.*, **52**, 273-380.

BRIM, O.G., GLASS, D.C., LAVIN, D.E., & GOODMAN, N., (1962). *Personality and Decision Processes.* Stanford: University Press.

EYSENCK, H.J. (1967). *The Biological Basis of Personality.* Springfield: Thomas.

EYSENCK, H.J., & EYSENCK, S.B.G. (1964). *Manual of the Eysenck Personality Inventory.* London: University Press.

FOULDS, G.A. (1951). Temperamental differences in maze performance I. Characteristic differences among psychoneurotics. *Brit. J. Psychol.*, **42**, 209-217.

GIBSON, H.B. (1969). The Gibson Spiral Maze Test. Retest data in relation to behavioural disturbance, personality and physical measures. *Brit. J. Psychol.*, **60**, 523-528.

HENDRY, L.B. (1970). A comparative analysis of student characteristics. M.Ed. thesis, University of Leicester.

HIMMELWEIT, H.T. (1946). Speed and accuracy of work as related to temperament. *Brit. J. Psychol.*, **36**, 132-144.

KAY, H. (1957). Information theory in the understanding of skills. *Occ. Psych.*, **31**, 218-224.

POULTON, E.C. (1965). Skill in the fast ball games. *Biology and Human Affairs*, **31**, 1-5.

SHANMUGAN, T.E. (1965). Personality, severity of conflict and decision time. *J.Ind. Acad. Appl. Psychol.*, **2**, 13-23.

SHARP. R.H. (1975). Input characteristics of ball skill acquisition. Unpublished Ph.D. thesis, University of Leeds.

SHARP, R.H. & WHITING, H.T.A. (1974). Exposure and occluded duration effects in a ball catching skill. *J. Motor Beh.*, **6**, 139-147.

WHITING, H.T.A. (1967). Visual motor co-ordination. Unpublished Ph.D. thesis. University of Leeds.

WHITING, H.T.A. (1969). *Acquiring Ball Skill: a psychological interpretation.* London: Bell.

WHITING, H.T.A. (1970). An operational analysis of a continuous ball throwing and catching task. *Ergonomics*, **13**, 445-454.

WHITING, H.T.A., GILL, E.B. & STEPHENSON, J.M. (1970). Critical time intervals for taking in flight information in a ball-catching task. *Ergonomics*, **13**, 265-272.

WHITING, H.T.A. & HUTT, J.W.R. (1972). The effects of personality and ability on speed of decision regarding the directional aspects of ball-flight. *J. Motor Beh.*, **4**, 89-97.

WHITING, H.T.A. & SHARP, R.H. (1974). Visual occlusion factors in a discrete ball catching task. *J. Motor Beh.*, **6**, 11-16.

Author Index

145

Subject Index